Managing Children's Behaviour

Sheila Riddall-Leech

Heinemann Educational Publishers
Halley Court, Jordan Hill, Oxford OX2 8EJ
Part of Harcourt Education
Heinemann is the registered trademark of
Harcourt Education Limited
© Sheila Riddall-Leech

First published 2003

08 07 06 05 04 03
10 9 8 7 6 5 4 3 2 1

British Library Cataloguing in Publication Data is available
from the British Library on request.

ISBN 0 435 45532 X

Designed by Artistix, Thame, Oxon
Typeset by 🖌 Tek-Art, Croydon, Surrey

Printed in the UK by Scotprint

Tel: 01865 888058 www.heinemann.co.uk

Contents

Acknowledgements

The author would like to acknowledge the encouragement and support of the staff at Heinemann, especially Mary James, Rachel Gear and Camilla Thomas.

Many of the case studies in the book are based on children and families that the author has encountered in her career, with names changed to maintain and respect confidentiality; so grateful thanks to children everywhere from whom I have learnt so much.

Finally thank you to all those I love for their support.

Sheila Riddall-Leech

The author and publisher would like to thank the following organisations and individuals for permission to reproduce photographs and copyright material:

Alamy page 86
Bubbles pages 18, 85 (bottom) and 87 (top)
Corbis pages 63 and 89
Gareth Boden pages 31, 118 and 129
Gerald Sunderland pages 57, 84 and 85 (top)
Haddon Davies pages 36, 43, 123, 127, 174, 189 and 199
John Walmsley pages 87 (bottom) and 167

Crown copyright material on pages 65 and 182 is reproduced under Class Licence Number CO1W0000141 with the permission of the Controller of HMSO and the Queen's Printer for Scotland.

Introduction

Caring for and bringing up children can be one of the most rewarding and fulfilling of professions, but it can at times be demanding as we cope with behaviour that could be described as challenging and which can push us to our limits. This book aims to help those of us who are involved with the care and education of children to understand more about children's behaviour.

Children do not arrive in the world pre-programmed to behave in a way that is acceptable to the society in which they live. As they grow and develop they progressively understand the rules of 'acceptable' behaviour. They learn how to respond and interact with others and how to adapt their behaviour when necessary. However, they do not do all of this unaided and need adults to help them develop and learn. It is therefore very important that we have an understanding of our role in helping children to learn appropriate behaviour.

The term 'behaviour management' is frequently used, but it does not and should not imply that we, the adults, impose our will and views on children in order to make them behave in ways that we find acceptable. Behaviour management is in many ways the appropriate response to any form of behaviour plus the appropriate management of the environment to minimise stress to everyone concerned. Children should be in an environment that empowers them; in other words, an environment that encourages them to behave in certain ways because they want to, not because someone else is attempting to make them.

This book attempts to follow the ABC model of behaviour management, that is antecedents, behaviour and consequences. The first part of the book, the antecedents, considers what we understand by the term 'behaviour', from both a historical and legal perspective, and how our differing views can affect and influence our understanding. This part also discusses ways that children learn about behaviour, some of the theoretical perspectives that influence our practice and how children's development and needs can affect their behaviour.

In the second part of the book, the behaviour and consequences, we consider how to deal with situations and behaviours that may cause concern, ways to empower children and the positive aspects of behaviour management. This part also considers the additional support that is available and ways of working in partnership with parents. The second part of the book links theory to practice, looking at strategies and the management of behaviour both in the home and in childcare and educational settings. Some of the more common forms of behaviour that cause concern will also be considered.

Throughout the book there are case studies to link theory to practice and provide practical suggestions of how others have dealt with certain situations. There are also 'think it over' sections to encourage you to consider a specific topic, idea or theory. All chapters have a section at the end for you to check your knowledge and understanding.

Part 1
Understanding behaviour – the antecedents

Chapter 1

What is behaviour?

Introduction – Defining behaviour

Behaviour is a complex concept and can mean many different things to many different people. This means that behaviour is just as much about how we act in certain social situations, such as saying 'thank you' or letting another person pass, as it is about arguing, distracting others, fighting, or using offensive language. Behaviour includes everything that we say or do that can influence or have an impact on another person. Human behaviour has an impact on every aspect of our lives at some time and can be influenced by many things, such as where we are, whom we are with and our understanding of the situation.

Although every individual will show a vast range of changing views, purposes and behaviours during their life, there will be certain stable core characteristics that tend to remain throughout. These characteristics are moulded by the experiences of childhood and the influence of the family. It is from these early experiences that children learn the social knowledge, behaviours and opinions that are valued by the society in which they live.

Across the world, children are looked after and brought up in many diverse ways and they will gradually learn the behaviour that is considered appropriate to the society in which they are living. Every society or culture has its own 'rules' and social boundaries, with ways of behaving that are considered to be acceptable or not acceptable. Within each society, each individual family unit, school or childcare setting can also have its own rules and boundaries, for example, parents wanting to know where their children are, or wearing a school uniform, or packing toys away when asked. Most societies want children to grow into healthy adults who will become functioning members of their society. In order to develop ways to help children gain social understanding, and therefore appropriate behaviour, it is important to try to have a good understanding of what makes children behave in the ways that they do.

This chapter is designed to give you a better understanding of how our views and values can influence our understanding of behavioural issues and will include:

◆ factors that may influence our views and values
◆ current thinking.

Values and behaviour

Analysing our views and values about behaviour

Before we can start to understand why children behave in a certain manner, it is important that we examine our own views and values about behaviour.

> **ACTIVITY – What are your views about behaviour?**
>
> Read the following statements and then decide if you agree with each one or not.
> ◆ *Children should not hit anyone.*
> ◆ *Parents, teachers and childcare workers are right to influence children and make sure that they behave in an acceptable way.*
> ◆ *If you want to live in my house, you must do as I say.*
> ◆ *Children should be seen and not heard.*
> ◆ *It is acceptable for advertisers to target young children to try to sell certain products.*
> ◆ *Politicians are entitled to campaign and try to persuade us to change our minds.*
> ◆ *People behave differently in groups than when on their own.*
>
> You may find it difficult to agree or disagree completely with some of these statements and perhaps you thought, 'Well it depends on…' Some of the statements may have provoked a stronger reaction than others. For example, you may be opposed to violence in any form and so are quite likely to agree strongly with the first statement. You may have a young child who has tried to persuade you, with pleading words, temper tantrums, tears and promises of being good, to buy the latest expensive toy advertised on television. You can't really afford the toy and so feel strongly about advertisers using children in this way. You will have reacted differently to each statement depending on your level of agreement. These reactions will have been formed by your upbringing and culture, your age, and all the other factors that form your values.
>
> If you have the opportunity, it would be useful to discuss some of the statements with other people and compare your views.
> ◆ *Compare and think about your different reactions to the statements.*
> ◆ *Can you think of some reasons why certain behaviours make you react in the way that you do?*

The important thing to remember is that it is unavoidable that we are influenced by our own beliefs and values, and we must recognise that our own views are just some among many. But if we are aware of our own views, we should be able to take these into account in our roles when working with children.

Factors that may influence our views and values

There are several factors that may influence our reactions and views about behaviour, as shown in the spidergram below. We will look at each one of these in turn.

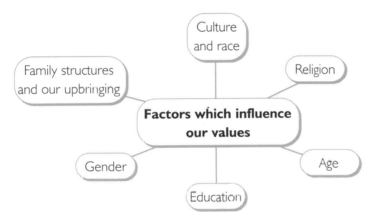

There are many influences on our views about behaviour

Family structures and our upbringing

The way that we were brought up affects our views about behaviour. We may have had authoritarian parents or carers who made rules about what we could or could not do, such as what time we had to be in at night, and when and where we could go out with friends. Some parents do not explain the reasons for the rules, believing that it is sufficient that the rule is there because they say so. We may have been the youngest child in the family, or the eldest or the only one; our position in the family and the way that we were treated by other family members influences our opinions and also affects how we in turn deal with our own children and those with whom we work.

In the same way, changes in family circumstances such as divorce, bereavement, abuse and ill health influence our opinions about certain behaviours; for example, if we have experienced major changes in our own family life, we may feel that we are more tolerant of, or understanding towards, children in similar circumstances who may not be behaving appropriately.

Finally, the financial conditions we have been used to in our upbringing does affect our judgements about acceptable behaviour. People tend to have strong feelings about wealth and poverty and may form firm opinions based on their view of someone's financial status.

Culture and ethnic group

Every culture and ethnic group has its own unique features that influence people. Our opinions on many issues, not only behaviour, are influenced and affected by our cultural traditions and heritage; for example, the clothes that we wear may have been influenced by our culture, as will where we want to go on holiday or our views on capital punishment. It might be quite common in one culture for children to behave in certain ways that other cultures might find unacceptable. Think about how this could affect our views and values.

Religion

Our religious views and beliefs can affect the way we conduct our lives now and in the future, as well as what has happened in the past. Our family's religious beliefs affect us as children and become part of our upbringing; this in turn affects our values today.

THINK IT OVER:

Consider the phrases: 'Turn the other cheek'; 'an eye for an eye'.

  I   How might these demonstrate contrasting values?

Age

People do not have the same opinions and values throughout their lives. Someone who was very tolerant when they were young might become much less so as they get older. Think of your own values. Have they changed? Do you have the same opinions as you had ten years ago?

Gender

Is it acceptable for boys and men to cry, or should the male sex hide their emotions and behave in ways that appear 'strong'? Our views about the way each gender should or should not behave obviously depends not only on our own gender, but also on our upbringing, family, ethnic group, culture and religion.

Education

It can be argued, following Piaget's theory (see page 20), that the more we learn about the world, the more able we are to construct ideas and concepts about our world. Thus learning influences our values in many ways.

Now consider your own views in connection with this case study.

CASE STUDY

Valerie and her older brother Robert were born in the 1950s. Their father worked in an office and their mother stayed at home. Father's word was 'law' and often the phrase, 'wait until your father gets home', was used by their mother when Valerie and Robert were not doing what their mother wanted them to do. The children were punished by being sent up to bed, irrespective of the time of day, or with a smack on the bottom. As the children got older their parents would only allow them to go out with friends on Friday and Saturday nights and they had to be in by 10 pm.

When Valerie had her own children she set 'rules' which were very different to those of her parents; for example, one rule was that once homework was finished the children could go out, provided they let their mother know where they were and what time they would be coming back. Valerie and her partner did not believe in smacking and preferred to use other ways to manage their children's behaviour. Valerie's parents thought that this was not a good idea; their view was that 'a smack didn't do you any harm, you let your children run rings around you'.

1   Do you agree with Valerie or her parents?

2   Can you think of anything that might have influenced your answer?

3   How did your parents deal with you when you were 'naughty'?

4   How has this affected the way you deal with the children that you care for or your own children?

Current thinking

As we have seen earlier in this chapter, many things may influence our views on behaviour. Ideas and thinking on behaviour are always being developed and modified. It is now widely believed that punishing children for actions that we might consider inappropriate is not effective. The current view is that punishments are negative. They do not consider the reasons for the behaviour and may make children lose confidence in themselves and their abilities. Current thinking suggests that children should be supported to enable them to learn how to manage their own behaviour. This is referred to as empowerment. Children should be encouraged to learn the skills and abilities to discipline themselves.

THINK IT OVER:

A lunchtime supervisor in a large primary school said that she would often shout at the children and appear cross and sometimes angry, when they were not 'playing properly', but it didn't seem to work. 'I now realise that the children didn't understand what the problem was. They thought that I was just a cross, bad-tempered dinner lady. I now try to talk to the children about how they are playing and suggest positive ways to make the situation better for everyone.'

Empowerment

If we really want what is best for children, we should be aiming to give them the skills and abilities to discipline themselves, and to encourage them to compromise voluntarily between what they want and what society demands; in this way, they can become empowered. Everyone needs some form of self-discipline in order to adjust their needs and desires to those of others and in order to be a complete and happy individual. This does not mean that one becomes self-centred or egotistical. Children need the affection and approval of people around them; they need to learn that they will not win this approval if they are selfish. In order to acquire the skills necessary for self-discipline or empowerment, it is necessary to allow a child to take control of certain situations. This could be in the form of offering a child more choices so that they can make decisions.

Empowerment is often associated with teaching children strategies to protect them from abuse. Empowerment is, however, more about developing confidence and positive self-esteem. These personal attributes can be contributory factors in a child's behaviour. If a child lacks confidence they may behave in inappropriate ways, such as withdrawing, or demonstrating behaviour normally associated with a younger child. Another way of helping children to be empowered is to help them to communicate effectively. A child with poor communication skills may feel that they are not in control of situations and this may provoke an adverse reaction. Helping children to express themselves in an appropriate way, to explain what they need or want and how they feel, is another way of empowering them.

Chapter 7 will look at empowerment in more detail. You may also want to look at Chapter 5, which considers how history has influenced our current laws and therefore our thinking about managing behaviour.

Another significant move in recent years has been the development of a multi-professional approach. This development has been prompted by The Children Act (1989). Those of us who work with children are now aware of the importance of multi-professional practices and the need to take into account a wide range of views of children. Health visitors, for example, are encouraged to extend their knowledge and expertise regarding individual children to large groups in a range of settings through programmes and initiatives such as Sure Start.

CHECKPOINT

1 What two things mould an individual's stable core characteristics?

2 List four factors that can influence our views and values.

3 Why is punishing children now not considered an effective method of behaviour management?

4 What is meant by empowerment?

5 Suggest a way that empowerment can be an effective tool for children.

6 What significant move in recent years has been prompted by the Children Act (1989)?

7 Name one initiative that uses a multi-professional approach.

Chapter 2

How behaviour is learnt

Introduction – Developmental theories and links to practice

We are not born as pre-programmed beings complete with all of the skills that we will need in life. We learn and develop these skills as we mature. Learning is an individual process for everyone and can take place in any situation, and at any age. Learning is not only about cognitive or intellectual growth and development but also includes knowing what responses may be appropriate in certain places and situations. There are many theories and points of view about how children learn. It is important that we have an understanding of these theories and views so that we can support children and help them to manage their own behaviour.

This chapter will consider three main categories of how children learn, and will link these theories to practice. The chapter will focus on:

◆ behaviourist theories

◆ social learning theory

◆ constructivist theories.

Many people believe that these different theories of how children learn complement each other rather than depict entirely different perspectives. The more we understand about theories of learning, the more we should be able to develop positive ways of helping and guiding children to manage their own behaviour.

Behaviourist theories

Classical conditioning

Classical conditioning was the first type of learning theory to be identified and studied, hence the name 'classical'. The major theorist in the development of classical conditioning is **Ivan Pavlov** (1849–1936), a Russian scientist trained in biology and medicine (as was his contemporary, Sigmund Freud). Pavlov was studying the digestive systems of dogs and became intrigued with his observation that when the older dogs were deprived of food, they began to salivate when one of his assistants walked into the room. He began to investigate this phenomenon and established the laws of classical conditioning.

Classical conditioning starts with a *reflex*, an innate, involuntary action or behaviour brought about or caused by an antecedent event (something that happens beforehand). In simple terms, if air is blown into your eye (antecedent event) you blink (a reflex). You have no voluntary or conscious control over whether the blink occurs or not. In the case of Pavlov's dogs the salivation is the reflex that helps the dogs digest food. The older dogs, however, did not salivate when the food was placed in front of them, but when the assistant came into the room. Pavlov deduced that the dogs had learnt to associate the assistant with being fed.

He decided to test this deduction further by ringing a bell when the food was given to the dogs. After this had happened a few times, Pavlov observed that the dogs had now learnt to associate the bell with food as they began to salivate when they heard the bell ringing in the absence of food.

Food arrives when the bell has rung

After some time the dog associates food with the bell ringing and salivates in preparation for eating – this is a conditioned response

Pavlov's dogs

Pavlov gave specific terms to the behaviours of the dogs and to explain his theory of classical conditioning. The box below explains these terms.

Dog sees food	→	Dog salivates
Unconditioned stimulus (UCS)	→	*Unconditioned response (UCR)*
Dog sees assistant	→	Dog salivates
Conditioned stimulus (CS)	→	*Conditioned response (CR)*
Dog hears bell, sees food	→	Dog salivates
CS + UCS	→	**UCR**
Dog hears bell	→	Dog salivates
CS	→	**CR**

Pavlov's theory of classical conditioning

Pavlov suggested that many biological responses in humans can be triggered by association. For example, in response to the baby suckling at the breast, impulses carried to the mother's pituitary gland cause the release of the hormone oxytocin. This causes milk to be 'let down' to the baby. Later, oxytocin may be released in response to the sight or sound of the baby, or as a result of preparation for breastfeeding. Some mothers may even experience 'let-down' to any baby's cry.

Pavlov also discovered that the conditioned response does not last forever, as in the case of his dogs; when the bell was rung, but no food appeared, the dogs eventually stopped salivating. This phenomenon is known as **extinction** as the conditioned response has been extinguished.

ACTIVITY

In many lactating mothers, the unconditioned response of the 'let down' reflex can become conditioned. Following the example given with Pavlov's dogs, write a sequence to show how this conditioning happens. The first part has been done for you.

Babies cries	→	Mother 'lets down' milk
Unconditioned stimulus (UCS)	→	*Unconditioned response (UCR)*

It is not only reflexes that can be conditioned. Emotions are strong responses and can be associated with a range of circumstances. For example, a piece of music or a song can trigger a strong feeling of happiness or sadness, depending on the circumstances that we associate with the music. A child might have been frightened by a dog barking and may learn to associate all dogs with a feeling of fear.

There is a well-documented experiment that was carried out by **John Watson** (1878–1958) in 1919–20, which attempted to prove Pavlov's theory. An eleven-month-old baby known as Albert was observed to play very happily with a white laboratory rat. This was regarded as a pleasurable experience for the baby. At the same time that Albert was playing, a sudden loud noise was made out of sight, which startled him and made him cry. After this was repeated a number of times, Albert began to cry whenever he saw the rat. He had become so conditioned that he was found to cry and show fear at anything that was soft and white.

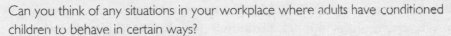

SEEING THEORY IN PRACTICE

This type of conditioning can be effective in many other situations. For example, a teacher might clap their hands and at the same time say to the class, 'Tidy-up time'. After a short while the teacher can stop saying the words and merely clap their hands to prompt the children to tidy up. The children have been conditioned to respond to the claps in a specific way.

THINK IT OVER:

Can you think of any situations in your workplace where adults have conditioned children to behave in certain ways?

1   How effective is the conditioning in getting the required response from the children?

2   What do you think might happen if the actions that resulted in the conditioning were stopped?

Operant conditioning

The theory of operant conditioning was established by **Edward Thorndike** (1874–1949). He is accredited with the Law of Effect which states:

If a response is followed by a satisfying, or pleasurable state of affairs or feelings it is more likely to be repeated. Other responses fade away.

For example, a child helps to tidy away and receives praise from an adult. This makes the child feel good and therefore more likely to want to help to tidy away again. Thorndike devised this Law of Effect after setting up an experiment with cats. A cat was put into a box from which it could escape by learning to operate a catch and lever. If the cat managed to escape it was rewarded with food. Thorndike observed that the cats learnt to escape by a process of trial and error and eventually they remembered how to escape and so get rewarded with food.

The theory is based upon the idea that changes in behaviour, or learning, are the result of an individual's response to events that occur in the environment. The theory was developed further by **B. F. Skinner** (1904–1990), who called these events **stimuli**. Skinner called the pleasant experiences **positive reinforcement**, showing how a pattern can be established:

Stimulus → Response → Positive reinforcement

Skinner developed the theory by also conducting experiments with animals, in this case, rats. Skinner devised a box with a lever and food tray inside. Pressing the lever released a food pellet into a tray and, like the cats in Thorndike's box, the rats soon learnt to press the lever to be rewarded with food.

Skinner's box

However, Skinner discovered that a number of things, apart from food or escaping, could act as rewards and not all animals responded in the same way to what Thorndike saw as pleasure giving. It seems fairly obvious that a well-fed rat is less likely to regard food as 'pleasure' than a starving one. Skinner used the term **reinforcer** to anything that could make the animal repeat the response. As well as positive reinforcers Skinner found that punishment often acted as a reinforcer. Sometimes the rats did not receive a food pellet, but got a mild electric shock. Skinner observed that if giving a response caused pain then the response soon disappeared. This he called **negative reinforcement**.

Skinner carried out a large number of experiments to try to find out the most effective reinforcers and whether the timing of reinforcement had any effect. He also established that reinforcers can be either primary, that is vital to life, such as food, or secondary, which are desirable things, such as money. For example, if we are hungry, we are more likely to respond to a stimulus that will satisfy our desire for food; and if we want money and are paid for doing something well, we will have a good reason for wanting to do it well again.

CASE STUDY

Katy takes money to school each day so that she can buy herself lunch. The school bully finds out that Katy has money and demands that she hands it over. When Katy refuses, the bully pulls her hair and hurts her. The bully continues to pull Katy's hair until she hands over the money. The next day the same thing happens. By the third day Katy hands over the money before the bully pulls her hair and so escapes the pain.

1 Was the reinforcement positive or negative?

2 Was it effective?

3 What has Katy learnt?

The main purpose of reinforcement is to shape behaviour in such a way that the behaviour will be repeated. Childcare workers frequently use verbal praise and smiles as positive reinforcers and angry expressions as negative reinforcers. Stickers, badges and treats are all forms of positive reinforcement. Skinner noticed that if reinforcement is given immediately, the behaviour is more likely to be repeated and learnt. For example, waiting until the evening to tell a child off for a misdemeanour that happened in the morning will not be as effective as dealing with it straightaway. (Remember Valerie and Robert in the earlier case study?)

Many professionals who subscribe to the operant conditioning theory are critical of the use of punishment. Punishment usually involves causing some kind of mental or physical distress by giving an unpleasant stimulus or withholding a pleasant one. It is believed by many that using reinforcements to increase acceptable behaviour is more effective than using punishment to decrease unacceptable behaviour.

THINK IT OVER:

For each of the following decide whether positive reinforcement, negative reinforcement or punishment is involved:

a   A bully pulls Katy's hair until she hands over her lunch money. When the bully has the money the hair pulling stops.

b   A three-year-old helps to tidy away the toys and his key-worker praises him and gives him a sticker.

c   Linton uses a swear word when playing. His mother says that he can't watch his favourite television programme later on.

d   A teacher encourages her class to tidy up quickly by promising extra story time.

e   A baby crawls over to another toddler and tries to take a toy. The toddler hits the baby. The key worker notices that the baby does not crawl near the toddler again.

SEEING THEORY IN PRACTICE

It is important to be aware that much research has been done in recent years on Skinner's theory. It has been shown that reinforcement is most effective when childcare workers and other professionals decide what behaviour they want from children and reinforce it when it occurs. It is important to tell the children what behaviour you want and that you tell them why you are praising them when they show the behaviour that you want. Research by **David Premack** (1965) showed that children can be encouraged to do something that they would prefer not to do by rewarding their behaviour with a more enjoyable activity. This has become known as the *Premack Principle*.

As well as different types of reinforcement, Skinner also identified five schedules of reinforcement:

1 **Continuous reinforcement** – the acceptable or desired behaviour is reinforced every time it happens, for example, every correct answer gets a tick; every time a child shows the desired behaviour they are praised.

2 **Fixed ratio** – the acceptable or desired behaviour is reinforced after a fixed number of times, for example, a toddler might be rewarded every other time he or she puts a toy away after playing with it, or three smiley face stickers wins a gold sticker.

3 **Variable ratio** – the acceptable or desired behaviour is reinforced as for fixed ratio, but every so often the number changes, so it could be every other time, then every fourth time, then every time, then back to every other. For example, a child is rewarded when sitting quietly at story time, but the child does not know when they will be rewarded, it could be every time, or after two incidences of sitting quietly.

4 **Fixed interval** – the acceptable or desired behaviour is reinforced after a set period of time, provided that there has been a correct response during that time, for example, children are rewarded for good behaviour at the end of every day.

5 **Variable interval** – the acceptable or desired behaviour is reinforced at variable times provided that there has been a correct response during that time. For example, children know that at some point during a day, or week, they will be rewarded if they behave appropriately, but they do not know at what point in the day or week this will be.

Studies have shown that when **continuous reinforcement** is used, children will learn more quickly, but once the behaviour is learnt, other forms of reinforcement can be used effectively to maintain the behaviour. If we want to teach a child a specific skill, it is usual to try to break down the skill into manageable steps. For example, we do not teach children to write words right at the start, we teach them how to hold writing materials, and let them make marks, then we may introduce shapes that they are familiar with and later recognisable letters. If each step is positively and continuously reinforced, research has shown that children will learn more effectively. This is usually referred to as *shaping*.

ACTIVITY

How would you encourage a child to learn how to brush their teeth correctly?

Work out how you could break down this skill into manageable steps, and write them down. Indicate on your plan when and how you could use reinforcement and what form that reinforcement might take.

Social learning theories

The social learning theory of **Albert Bandura** (born 1925) emphasises the importance of observing and modelling the behaviour, attitudes and emotional reactions of others. Bandura accepted the work of Pavlov, Thorndike and Skinner, but was not completely convinced that these were the only ways that children learnt. Bandura thought that children also learnt by observing and watching others; he called this **observational learning**.

Bandura was also concerned that other theorists had based their work on studies of animals, rather than of humans. Bandura believed that children can be selective in who they decide to copy and the reasons that they choose to copy certain behaviours.

Bandura tested this theory with a famous experiment in 1965 in which he showed three groups of nursery children a short film with three different endings. In the film the children saw an adult hitting an inflatable plastic doll (known as a Bobo doll) with a mallet, knocking the doll over, sitting on it and throwing things at it, whilst using aggressive language. The first group of children saw the ending where another adult came into the room and gave the first adult sweets for such a good performance. The second group saw the adult being told off and smacked for being aggressive and the third group did not see any reward or punishment.

After watching the film the children were allowed to play with the Bobo doll and some of the things that the adult had used to hit the doll with were left in the room. Bandura observed the behaviour of the children and noted that the children who saw the adult being punished were less aggressive than either of the other two groups. The group that saw the adult being praised and the group that saw neither punishment nor reward copied the behaviour of the adult and were equally aggressive. Bandura found that the aggressive model influenced the behaviour of the children in two ways: firstly it taught them new ways of being aggressive, but secondly it increased the number of times the children were aggressive in numerous ways, not just in relation to their play things.

In observational learning, the behaviour is more likely to be copied if the child sees the person modelling the behaviour being rewarded. This is known as **vicarious reinforcement**. An example of this is a childcare worker who sees a child behaving inappropriately, but purposefully praises another child who is behaving appropriately. The theory is that the first child sees the other child being rewarded and so will copy that behaviour.

In social learning theory another form of reinforcement is considered, apart from positive and negative in the operant conditioning theory. This is known as **intrinsic reinforcement**, whereby the reinforcement comes from within the person, such as satisfaction at a job well done, or learning a new skill, or a sense of pride and achievement. This can be a very powerful form of reinforcement, as ultimately we want children to behave in appropriate ways because *they* want to and not because *we* want them to.

Role models

Bandura believed that if children are to learn by observation, they must study the model quite closely and some models are more worth looking at than others. The models who have the most influence are people who are warm and loving towards the child or people who have more power, influence or skill, and people who are similar to themselves, or the same gender or age. These people are usually referred to as **role models**. Some of these role models are more important to a child at different ages than at other times. For example, young children copy the way their parents or carers talk and do certain things – such as watching an adult shape play dough and then making the same shapes as the adult. Older children on the other hand choose role models from their peer group and adult influence becomes less important.

Children copy adults' behaviour from an early age!

> ### SNAPSHOT
>
> Jenni has worked in a large day nursery for several years. When she wants the children to tidy toys away, or to stop doing something she considers unacceptable, she shouts in a very loud voice. At a staff meeting another member of staff says that he feels that some of the children are getting very noisy and often use raised voices to each other. The staff discuss ways that they could lower the noise level in the nursery and decide that one thing they will all do is only to use normal speaking voices at all times. After a few days the noise level in the nursery has dropped. Jenni admits that she did not realise that she was shouting as much as she had been and obviously the children were copying her.

Role models are not always good or positive. Bandura's theory also explains why children may be influenced by the media; for example, a child may see a famous footballer spit during a game, or argue with the referee. A child who sees these well-known personalities behaving in this way may believe it is acceptable and copy them. Can you think of role models that you have had in the past who influenced you to behave in a certain way? Was that influence positive or negative, or did it depend on who you were with?

Learning by observation

Why is it that we cannot become skilled footballers or musicians simply by watching and observing people like David Beckham or Elton John? Bandura accepted that it is too naïve to think that we can automatically copy someone's behaviour by watching them and become as skilled as the model. According to the social learning theory, there are five processes involved in observational learning. These are:

1 **Motivation** – a person must want to copy certain behaviour, in order to be rewarded or for reasons of intrinsic motivation, such as satisfaction, pleasure.

2 **Attention** – a person needs to pay close attention to what the role model is doing and be able to ignore behaviour or actions that are not related to the behaviour. For example, a child who wants to copy an adult washing their hands will have to ignore the fact that the adult could be singing as they wash their hands and pay attention only to the actions that relate to hand-washing.

3 **Practice** – the first time a child tries to copy their role model, they may not get the behaviour quite right, so they may need to try again. In this process the memory plays an important part.

4 **Memory** – a person copying must store the information that they have seen, in order to copy it.

5 Once the behaviour has been stored in the memory it may need to be considered or **revisited** fairly often, so that it is not forgotten.

CASE STUDY

The staff at a day nursery noticed that the number of children with coughs and colds had increased. They decided to focus children's attention on good hygiene practices, such as washing hands after going to the toilet or before eating a meal, and covering the mouth when coughing or sneezing, to try to reduce the chances of spreading infection. The staff made deliberate, purposeful comments to the children such as, 'I am just going to the toilet and then I will wash my hands.' They made sure that when they coughed or sneezed they covered their own mouths and made an appropriate comment afterwards to children nearby and praised each other for doing 'the right thing'. The adult being praised made a point of showing their pleasure at receiving the praise. Within a few days the children had begun to imitate these good hygiene practices.

1 In terms of social learning theory, how could you explain why the children had begun to imitate the day nursery staff?

2 Why was it important that the adults were heard to praise each other?

3 What other types of behaviour might children copy from early years and childcare workers?

THINK IT OVER:

There is no doubt that social learning, or observational learning theory, is a very powerful way of helping children to learn. However, some scientists claim that it is our genes that determine certain characteristics, such as aggression, not always role models. For example, in the case of aggressive and violent children with aggressive and violent parents, have the children learnt to behave in that way through social learning or are those characteristics inherited? It must be remembered that all children are unique and see role models differently, and might therefore interpret the behaviour in various ways.

Constructivist theories

Some educationalists call this group **cognitive theories**. The term *constructivist* is attributed to **Jean Piaget** (1896–1980), who described himself as a constructivist and believed that learning is about building on new experiences and modifying old experiences in order to develop new knowledge. In the previous theories discussed in this chapter, children learn due to things happening to them, such as receiving rewards. Constructivists such as Piaget, **Bruner** and **Vygotsky** believe that children learn from their own actions and from exploring their own environment.

Piaget spent much of his professional life studying children and so developed his theory of **cognitive development**. It is this theory that has influenced much of the way in which young children are taught.

Piaget's theory identified four aspects of cognitive development:

1 **Schema** – schemas are early ideas or concepts based on linked patterns of behaviour and are part of a child's powerful drive to understand his or her experiences. Piaget noticed that children habitually gave the wrong answers to questions in an intelligence test. He kept a record of these answers and discovered over a period of years that these answers were not haphazard, but did in fact follow a logical pattern based on the children's own conclusions developed from their experiences. Piaget called these conclusions schemas. Schemas develop from active exploration of the environment. Piaget believed that in the early stages, children explore their environment using their senses; therefore early schemas are a result of sensory development and stimulation. For example, a crawling baby, touching with hands and tongue, and looking intently at an empty coffee mug, can develop a schema that all coffee mugs are cold and hard. If the baby crawls over to a mug that contains hot coffee and touches it, the schema will be changed, or developed as a result of this sensory experience.

2 **Assimilation** – Piaget believed that children are able to adapt their schemas when they have a new experience. This process is called **assimilation**.

Assimilation happens when a child finds that an existing schema fits another circumstance. It involves the taking in of information about objects or people in the child's environment. A child may for example find that the schema for holding a rattle can also be used for holding a piece of toast.

3 **Accommodation** – accommodation is when a child realises that their schema does not fit or match the situation that they are in, or what is happening around them. This results in the child developing a new schema.

4 **Equilibrium/disequilibrium** – there must be a balance between assimilation and accommodation. The child must not take in more than they can practise, use and come to understand. Piaget called this balance **equilibrium**. Too much information or stimulation causes confusion, because the child has not been able to accommodate existing information. Piaget called this confusion **disequilibrium**.

SEEING THEORY IN PRACTICE

Four-year-old Amir is playing with a construction set. He already has a schema for doing this, which is based on his past experiences of playing. He knows that he has to look at the pieces and work out what to do first. This is *assimilation*. However, some of the pieces do not fit together in the way that Amir expects, so he is put into a mental state of *disequilibrium*. He now has to adjust his schema about the construction set to take in the information that not all the pieces fit together in exactly the same way. This is *accommodation*. Amir is able to build a model using the new schema that the different pieces fit together in different ways. This is a cognitive, or constructivist explanation of how Amir learnt to fit different pieces of his construction set together.

Piaget's work continues to be debated and discussed, but some educationalists feel that Piaget's explanations are too simplistic. Piaget believed that children pass through different and distinctive stages in their cognitive development; but if they are continually assimilating and accommodating information, some would argue that children's development is continuous. There has been much recent research on how schemas develop. In 1990 **Chris Athey** did extensive research in this area and suggested that schemas do not develop independently but that children need other children and adults in order to learn.

The influence of other people

An extension of the constructivist theory considers the influence of other people on children's learning and is usually referred to as the **social constructivist model**. **Jerome Bruner** (born 1915) and **Lev Vygotsky** (1896–1934) have both researched this influence.

Bruner developed the term **scaffolding**, where adults or indeed other children can help to make a child's learning more manageable – especially when they are learning something new. An example of this might be helping a child to learn how to feed themselves by offering food that is easy to pick up with fingers, or helping a child to solve a problem by asking questions that will guide the child to a solution.

THINK IT OVER:

It could be argued that there are distinct similarities between scaffolding and shaping. Can you suggest why?

Vygotsky believed that social interaction was a fundamental part of children's learning. He supported the view that children learn by interacting with their environment, but believed that an adult or more able child could take the learning much further than when they are learning in isolation. He called the difference between what a child could learn on their own and that which they could learn with the help of others the **zone of proximal development**. (This is often referred to as the ZPD.)

SEEING THEORY IN PRACTICE

Each year as GCSE results are announced the media run stories of young children achieving these qualifications at a very early age. These children would not be able to do this unless they had received appropriate adult help and support, thus operating in the zone of proximal development.

CHECKPOINT

1   What is meant by the classical conditioning theory? Name one theorist.

2   What is a reflex action?

3   Define the term 'extinction' and name the theory it is associated with.

4   Explain how shaping could be used to teach a child how to play a musical instrument.

5   What theory would support the view that adults need to be good role models for children?

6   What are the five processes involved in observational learning?

7   What is meant by cognitive theory? Give an example of one theorist.

8   Define the term 'schema' and give an example.

9   What is the Zone of Proximal Development?

Chapter 3

More theoretical perspectives

Introduction – More developmental theories and links to practice

Chapter 2 looked at the ways that children can learn, but learning is just one aspect of a child's overall development. All aspects of a child's development and learning are interlinked, for example, a difficulty with the use of language could lead to the child feeling emotionally frustrated which could in turn affect how they react in certain situations. This chapter will look at theoretical perspectives and theories on:

◆ social and emotional development

◆ attachment and separation

◆ moral development

◆ the self-fulfilling prophecy.

Social and emotional development

Social development is about learning to be with other people, how to build relationships and how to make friends. It also about knowing how to look after ourselves and acquiring self-help skills, such as independent toileting and getting dressed. Emotional development is about how we learn to deal with our feelings. It is about how children bond with their carers or make strong bonds with a small number of adults. This aspect of development is also about the development of self-confidence, self-control, self-image and personality. It is often difficult to separate emotional development from social development as aspects of one affect the other. Both of these areas of development can be powerful influences on how a child behaves. It is therefore important that we understand the theoretical perspectives that attempt to explain these developmental areas.

Theorists such as **Sigmund Freud** (1856–1939) and **Erik Erikson** (1902–1994) believed that a baby under the age of three months is incapable of true emotion. This is because of the close links between emotional and social development. Many types of emotion, such as delight, love, anger and jealousy depend upon social awareness – a consciousness of self and of others. Social awareness is not present in a newborn child, but develops gradually from the child's interactions with his or her family, main carers and those with whom they have contact. It is true that a young baby will appear to scream with anger or rage, especially when hungry, or if its other physiological needs are not met, but can this be described as an emotional outburst? Babies are born with some basic capabilities and distinct temperaments, which in turn affect how others react and respond to them. However, their capabilities and temperaments go through considerable changes as they mature and develop social awareness. Both Freud and Erikson were theorists whose work is often linked to possible explanations of how personality develops. Many people believe that personality is a key factor in how a person behaves and this will affect how an individual comes to terms with stressful or emotional times in their lives. Many childcare workers will be able to identify situations where some circumstances do not appear to have adversely affected a child, such as a hospital stay, or the breakdown of a relationship within the family, whilst other children will show disturbed behaviour patterns in the same circumstances.

Freud, in particular, was very interested in how behaviour can be affected and influenced by unconscious thoughts, or instinctive urges. Freud put forward the theory that our actions are motivated by two instincts. The first he called the **libido**, a positive force that gives an individual the energy and the need to survive; and the second, the **death wish**, which is a negative force controlling aggression and other negative actions and emotions. Freud believed that the personality of an individual was affected by the balance between the libido and the death wish. Every individual has libido, but each person has different experiences and is brought up in different ways, which accounts for different personalities. Libido makes individuals behave in ways that relieve pressures that would otherwise build up. When the libido is frustrated, emotional problems can occur. The death wish is destructive and makes some people want to dominate others; it can make people want to put themselves in dangerous situations, and even want to cause harm to people they dislike or hate. Freud suggested that children should 'take out' these aggressive, angry feelings on toys, objects or furniture and that if these feelings are not realised some personality problems will occur later in life. Freud suggested that in 'healthy' individuals, the libido should be more powerful than the death wish.

Freud's studies led him to suggest that personality consists of three related elements, the first being the **id**, which leads to the **ego** and finally the third part, the **superego**. The id exists from birth and is the most basic part of the personality. Freud described the id as irrational as a child is only concerned and interested in things which give pleasure; it is not of the 'real world'. The id is concerned with survival needs. The id must be satisfied *now*, for example, a baby screams with 'rage' because it is hungry. Freud believed that some people may continue to have a dominant id throughout their lives.

The ego develops around the ages of two to three years, as children start to develop language skills and begin to learn that they have to ask for some things. The id is still making irrational demands, but the child has learnt that some demands are more realistic than others; the ego is more of the 'real world'. It is rational and logical and allows a child to understand that talking, explaining, negotiating and asking will be more effective ways to satisfy the demands of the id; for example, a child asks for a biscuit or snack before a meal because they are hungry. The ego works out ways to satisfy the id.

The development of the superego is seen when 'moral reasoning', or the understanding of the differences between right and wrong, develops. The superego makes sure that the ego does not ask for, or do, unacceptable things in order to satisfy the demands of the id. It is effectively a kind of moral personality censor. The superego prompts such thoughts as, 'You can't have it, or do it, because it is wrong'; for example, the superego would stop a hungry child stealing food before a mealtime after a request for a biscuit has been refused, because stealing is wrong.

SEEING THEORY IN PRACTICE

Freud believed that very early childhood experiences are responsible for how people think and feel in later life. An example of this might be the effects of attempting potty-training before a child is developmentally ready, or carrying it out inflexibly and harshly. Freud would have us believe that this can lead to a child becoming a person who hates mess, is obsessively tidy, organised, punctual and respectful of authority.

Erikson was a student of Freud and was greatly influenced by his work. Erikson believed that development occurs in stages and like Freud believed that issues from earlier stages can affect later development. However, Erikson felt that the stages of development are linked to cognitive and social development as opposed to Freud's belief that development is led by physical needs. Erikson's theory supports the belief that if a young child, in the early stages of development, is repeatedly told that they are bad or useless, they may when older never try very hard to develop new skills as they will not think that they are able or that they possess any worth, i.e. they will have very low self-esteem.

CASE STUDY

After a hard labour and difficult birth, Karin gave birth to a healthy baby, but found it very hard to respond to him as she blamed the child for her pain and depression. Karin remained unresponsive towards the baby as he grew older, often belittling his actions or attempts at independence. He did not become fully potty trained until he was almost five. She would often describe her son as a 'load of trouble', 'a pain', or 'useless'. When the boy began school he often refused to try anything new, such as learning to use scissors, as he thought that he could not cut out 'properly'. He became very distressed when asked to perform in the infant class Christmas play as he said that he couldn't remember the words of the songs. It was obvious to staff that he had very poor self-esteem and lacked confidence in his own abilities.

1 How do you think this case study supports Erikson's theory?

2 What do you think staff could do to help Karin's son develop self-confidence?

Erikson suggested that all individuals pass through eight psychosocial stages, with each stage characterised by a different psychological 'crisis' which must be resolved before the individual can move on to the next stage. If the individual does not cope with the crisis in an effective manner, the outcome will be more struggles with that issue later in life. Erikson's stages are set out in the table below.

Stage	Age (approx)	Crisis	Description	Positive outcomes	Negative outcomes
1	Infancy 0–1 yr (Oral/sensory)	Trust versus mistrust	Infants depend on others around them to meet their basic needs, therefore they have to decide if the people around them are trustworthy or not.	If their needs are met consistently and responsively, secure attachments will develop and babies learn to trust their environment as well.	If their needs are not met, babies will develop mistrust towards people and things in their environment and themselves.
2	Toddler 1–2 yrs (Muscular/anal)	Autonomy (independence) versus doubt and shame	Toddlers learn to walk, talk, get control of bladder and bowel and do things for themselves. Self-confidence and control is beginning to develop.	If parents/carers encourage the child's use of initiative and reassure them when they make mistakes, the child will develop the confidence needed to cope with future situations that require choice, control and independence.	If parents/carers are overprotective or disapproving of the child's acts of independence, he or she may begin to feel ashamed of their behaviour, or begin to doubt their own abilities.

▶

Stage	Age (approx)	Crisis	Description	Positive outcomes	Negative outcomes
3	Early childhood 3–6 yrs (Locomotor)	Initiative versus guilt	Children have new-found power as they develop physical skills and become more engaged in social interactions. They must learn to achieve a balance between the need for more adventure and the need for more responsibility, and learn to control impulses and childish fantasies.	If parents/carers are consistent with discipline, children will learn to accept, without guilt, that certain things are not allowed, but at the same time will be able to feel guilt when engaging in imaginative and role-play.	If consistency is not present, children may develop a sense of guilt and may come to believe that it is wrong to be independent.
4	Middle school years 6–12 yrs (Latency)	Competence versus inferiority	School is the important event at this stage. Children learn to make things, use tools and acquire the skills to be a worker and potential provider, at the same time making the transition from home to the world of peers.	If children discover pleasure in intellectual stimulation, being productive and seeking success, they will develop a sense of competence.	If children do not discover pleasure in this way, they will develop a sense of inferiority.
5	Adolescence 13–18 yrs	Identity versus confusion	'Who am I?' To answer this successfully Erikson suggests that the adolescent must have resolved all earlier conflicts and so be ready for this 'identity 'crisis. Erikson considers this the most significant conflict a person must face.	If this conflict is successfully resolved he or she will emerge from this stage with a strong identity and ready to plan for the future.	If the crisis is not resolved he or she will sink into confusion, unable to make decisions and choices, especially about sexual orientation, future studies and employment.
6	Young adult 19–40 yrs	Intimacy versus isolation	The most important events are love relationships. An individual who has not developed a sense of identity will fear a committed relationship and may may retreat into isolation.	Adults can form close intimate relationships and share with others if they have achieved a sense of identity.	If the sense of identity is not formed, adults will fear commitment, feel isolated and unable to depend on anybody.
7	Middle adulthood 40–65 yrs	Generativity versus stagnation	By 'generativity' Erikson means the adult's ability to look outside oneself	People can resolve this crisis by having and nurturing children or by	If this crisis is not successfully resolved, the person will remain

Stage	Age (approx)	Crisis	Description	Positive outcomes	Negative outcomes
7 (cont.)			and care for others, through parenting, for example. Erikson suggests that adults need children as much as children need adults.	helping the next generation.	self-centred and may experience stagnation later in life.
8	Maturity 65 to death	Ego integrity versus despair	Old age is a time for reflection, and seeing one's life filled with pleasures, satisfactions, or disappointment and failures.	If the adult has achieved a sense of fulfilment about life he or she will accept death with a sense of integrity. Just as the healthy child will not fear life, Erikson said the healthy adult will not fear death.	If fulfilment is not achieved, the individual will despair and fear death.

Erikson's stages of psychosocial development

Self-esteem – how we see ourselves

For many people, self-esteem and self-confidence are almost the same thing, because how confident we feel depends on how much we like ourselves. Having a good sense of self-esteem or being confident is important because it means that we are more likely to be able to try out new things, make new friends and take the initiative in situations. Having low self-esteem or lacking confidence means that we may never meet our full potential. We saw in the case study of Karin and her son how his low self-esteem stopped him from trying out new things. In the same way, children sometimes display inappropriate behaviours because they are afraid of trying hard and failing. Sometimes we may interpret this as a child deliberately 'misbehaving'. Self-esteem will be looked at in more detail in Chapter 4.

CASE STUDY

Jake is ten years old and goes to an after-school club. He is playing table tennis with three other children. The first time the ball comes on to his side of the table he misses it. Jake is very aware that his friends can all hit the ball with their bats and that he can't. His partner starts to complain that they are going to lose the game. Finally Jake slams his bat forcefully on to the table and walks off.

1 Why do you think Jake reacted in this way?

2 What do you think the play worker could do to help Jake?

Self-concept

As our personality develops, so does the way we see ourselves; this is our self-image or self-concept. Our self-concept is not just about what we see when we look at ourselves in a mirror. It is concerned with what sort of person we believe ourselves to be. Self-concept is also about how we think other people see us and what we would like to be. This idea is often referred to as our 'ideal self' and does not just mean the dream that we could lose several pounds in weight or win the lottery. The way we see ourselves is influenced by personality traits, for example, do you see yourself as shy and introverted or as an extrovert and the life and soul of the party? Self-image can be influenced by parental expectations, for example, it may be very important to a child's parents that their child achieves the highest possible level in the school Standard Assessment Tests (SATs), because they want the 'best' for their child. The child, on the other hand, may feel under pressure to achieve this and, if they do not, may see themselves as 'letting their parents down', or not being good enough.

Self-image is also influenced by the roles we have in life, such as our role within our family: depending on whose company we are in, are we mothers, daughters, brothers, or uncles? There are also professional roles, such as being a student, early years worker, or teacher. We may also have roles in our leisure time or in relation to community involvement. In addition, our age, gender, physical characteristics, religion, culture and ethnic origin all contribute to our roles in society. Clearly, the influences upon an individual's self-image are numerous.

ACTIVITY

Try writing a realistic description of how you see yourself and your personality traits. Then ask someone who knows you well to do the same and compare the two descriptions. You will probably find that there are differences in the two descriptions as no two people see things in exactly the same way. Also your description of yourself will be influenced by where you are at the time of writing, who you are with, your family, your age, gender and other environmental factors.

Attachment theory

Bowlby's theory of attachment

John Bowlby (1907–1990) was one of the first researchers to study relationships between young babies and children and their mothers or primary carers. Bowlby developed the theory of **attachment**, which focused on the emotional tie between a child and another person, usually an adult. Bowlby's work has greatly influenced social care policy, childcare practices and research since the

1950s. More recently there has been some criticism of his work, centring on aspects which are mainly due to the social and political climate at the time of Bowlby's early research when mothers were the primary caregivers; however, Bowlby's later research emphasised that babies could form attachments with someone other than the mother. There is little doubt that if children are to have good social relationships as they grow and develop, it is important that they have had positive relationships with their parents or carers as babies.

SEEING THEORY IN PRACTICE

As a direct result of Bowlby's research and work, hospitals changed many of their practices. Today it is regarded as good practice that as soon as possible after giving birth a mother is encouraged to hold her baby. This enables a bond to develop between the mother and baby and is essential if the baby's basic survival needs are to be met.

Developing positive attachments

A mother may miss out on the initial bonding process and interactions with her baby if, for example, she or her baby are ill. However, they can still go on to develop a positive attachment. Repeated interactions between mother and baby ensure that the bonding process and attachments are strong. The quality of these interactions can influence a child's behaviour when they are older. Mothers who are insensitive to their baby's needs and do not, or are unable to, respond appropriately tend to have babies who are unsettled and may display unusual attachment behaviour as they grow and develop.

It is important to remember that the bonding between a mother and her baby does not mean round-the-clock care by the mother of her baby. It does not mean that mothers who work and have another person caring for their baby at certain times of the day do not have secure bonds and attachments with their baby, or that the baby will develop behaviour problems in later life. It is more important that the interactions between a mother and her baby when they are together are of good quality. A loving working mother who can enjoy the company of her child after a day at work will often have a less stressful and fraught relationship with the child than the mother who feels resentful because she is 'stuck at home' or, for example, is anxious and worried about money and living within very restricted financial means.

Bowlby put forward the theory that failure to make a bond or attachment with the mother in infancy may lead to serious problems, such as juvenile delinquency, later in life. This raised the very important question as to whether mothers should go out to work or stay at home and look after the children. However, further studies of a more cross-cultural nature contradict Bowlby's theory. For example, in Israeli kibbutzim, children are cared for by a professional child-nurse, a 'metapelet', and only visit their parents at the end of the working day. In many cultures and societies, grandparents or aunts and uncles care for children whilst their parents are at work. Grandparents and other family members may play a significant role in helping children develop strong social relationships. Frequently, children who are cared for by family members other than their parents feel secure as they have built relationships with their extended family.

The role of fathers

Bowlby emphasised that fathers may become attached to their babies in very much the same way as mothers. However, research has shown that the interactions between the baby and each parent may be very different. Mothers generally talk and smile at the babies more and use a quieter tone of voice. Fathers tend to be more physical, especially as the baby develops and grows. The behaviour of fathers might be influenced by their own fathers' behaviour, or through images of fathers that they have seen around them and in the media. These differences in the interactions between parents and children have an influence on the learning and behaviour of the child.

Bonding with a father/carer can be a valuable relationship

THINK IT OVER:

Spend a few moments watching the children with whom you work playing outside.

Make a note of any differences you can see between the way that the girls play and the way that the boys play.

Do you think that any differences you can see might reflect the different ways in which mothers and fathers interact with their children?

ACTIVITY

We can learn a huge amount about children from observing them in different situations. Watch children when they are greeting a parent and fill out the chart below. Then try to answer the questions which follow. You might want to do this activity several times to get as broad a picture as possible.

Gender of child	Which parent/carer?	Language used	Physical contact and what it was
Child 1			
Child 2			
Child 3			
Child 4			
Child 5			

1 Did you notice any difference between the way mothers and fathers (or male and female carers) greeted their sons or male charges?

2 Did you notice any difference between the way mothers and fathers (or male and female carers) greeted their daughters or female charges?

3 Did you notice any difference between the type of physical contact between mothers and fathers/carers and their sons or male charges?

4 Did you notice any difference between the type of physical contact between mothers and fathers/carers and their daughters or female charges?

5 Did you notice any differences in the behaviour of the children towards their mothers or fathers/carers?

6 From your own knowledge and using the information that you have already read, can you suggest possible reasons for some of the differences that you have observed?

Effects of separation

Separation, the opposite in many ways of attachment, may affect and influence the ways in which a child behaves. Much research has been carried out on the effects of separation, in particular, the work of **James** and **Joyce Robertson** in the 1960s and 1970s. They carried out several well-documented studies of children who had been separated from their parents for a variety of reasons. The results of the Robertsons' work led to major changes in hospital policies regarding hospitalised children and their parents. For example, it is now expected that the parent of a young child who has to have an operation will stay in hospital with them.

Stages of separation

Each child reacts differently to being separated from their parents or from the adult with whom they have strong and positive attachments; however, researchers have been able to identify distinct stages that children may go through when separated. Initially children will *protest*. This can be seen quite clearly, for example, when a parent leaves a child at nursery and the child kicks, struggles, cries, screams and shows distress. Protest is usually followed by *despair*, when the child may appear to have calmed down and be submissive. Often the child will reject offers of comfort from other adults and will attempt to comfort themselves by rocking or sucking their thumb. Finally, the child seems to be *detached*, and tries to make relationships with other adults. When the adult from whom the child was separated returns the child may reject them.

The behaviour of separated children is influenced by several factors, including the length of the separation, their previous experiences, whether the separation was planned or unexpected and the age of the child. Studies have also shown that boys tend to be more distressed than girls, and that the behaviour of children who have not developed positive social relationships is influenced more strongly by separations.

Divorce and separation

Separations can happen at any time in a child's life; they can be planned, such as a hospital stay, or unplanned such as the breakdown of the parents' relationship. In the latter case, a child may become separated from either their father or mother for periods of time. As the divorce rate in Britain has soared, psychologists have been interested in the effects that divorce may have on children and this has been the subject of much research. Freud argued that the absence of a father during a young son's personality development would have devastating consequences for the child's personality. Other psychologists believe that children who learn by observing and copying their parents will miss out on a vital source of information if one parent is absent. In this case children may not understand or learn about the differences in the behaviour of one or other gender.

Research has shown that the influence of divorce is greater on boys than on girls, especially if the father is absent during the pre-school years.

CASE STUDY

Paul's parents divorced when he was five years old and he spent the rest of his childhood and teenage years living with his mother, sister and grandmother. During his late teens and early twenties, Paul had several relationships with girls before setting up home with his girlfriend. He had few friends of the same sex, always saying that he felt more comfortable in the company of females. Paul and his partner now have two children, both boys. Paul found it very difficult to establish a relationship with his first son; he did not know how fathers should behave, what sort of language they should use; and his partner felt that he expected too much of his son. When the second child was born, Paul thought that he might do 'better' with this child, but he still had difficulties. This put a strain on his relationship with his partner and eventually Paul sought counselling. It was suggested that he tried to develop relationships with males of all ages, but unfortunately Paul does not know where to start.

1 Why do you think Paul can't relate to his sons?

2 If you were Paul's partner, how might you help him?

3 How do you think his sons may react?

It is estimated that nearly 30 per cent of all children born in the United Kingdom in the twenty-first century are likely to experience their parents separating before they reach school-leaving age. Many people tend to assume that children from broken homes and relationships are at a disadvantage in life, and will suffer from emotional or behavioural problems. It is true that some children will suffer in this way but it is also a fact that many overcome their grief and the disruption of an intimate relationship and grow up to be ordinary, contented members of society.

In some ways, the effects of having a parent in prison are very much the same as those experienced by a child whose parents have separated or divorced. Children may be separated from their main carer and may be too young to fully understand the implications of the separation. Sometimes these situations put other family members under stress, causing emotional difficulties, and this will affect and influence the behaviour of the children.

Moral development

Moral development is often grouped with social and emotional development, as many believe it is an important part of the socialisation process. Piaget studied children as they played and observed how they develop rules and a concept of 'right and wrong'. He came to the conclusion that children's moral development is linked to their cognitive development.

Lawrence Kohlberg (1927–1987) is well known for his work on moral development in the early 1970s. His theory was based on Piaget's conclusions and those of American philosopher John Dewey. Kohlberg believed (and was able to show through studies) that people progress in their moral reasoning through a series of stages. He believed that there are six identifiable stages that can be more generally grouped into three levels, as shown in the chart below.

Level	Stage	Social orientation
Pre-conventional (Approximate ages: 6–13 yrs)	1	Obedience and punishment – we do what we are told to do by a figure of authority, for example, obeying a teacher who tells us to sit down.
	2	Individualism, instrumentalism and exchange – we do what we think is in our own best interests, for example, tidying our room when asked in order to have more time to play outside with our friends.
Conventional (Approximate ages: 13–16 yrs)	3	'Good boy/girl' – we do what we think is acceptable to society (hence the name conventional), for example, saying please and thank you at appropriate times in order to gain the approval of others, such as our parents and/or carers.
	4	Law and order – we do things that will not break the law, for example, not stealing.
Post-conventional (Approximate ages: 16 yrs+)	5	Social contract – we do things in response to an understanding of social mutuality, and an empathy/affinity with others, leading to a genuine interest in the welfare and support of others, for example, caring for an ill person in order to alleviate the symptoms of their illness. At this level we can be forced to choose between moral values and the law, for example, should we break the law by stealing money in order to buy illegal drugs that will alleviate the symptoms of a person's illness?
	6	Principled conscience – we do what we think our conscience is telling us is the 'right' thing to do in principle, for example, caring for an ill person because we believe in preserving and respecting life.

Kohlberg's stages of moral development

The first level of thinking is found at primary and early secondary school level – children behave according to socially acceptable norms because they are told to do so by some authority figure (this links with Erikson's Stage 4 of emotional development). The second stage of this level is characterised by a view that behaviour means acting in one's own best interests.

The second level of moral thinking is characterised by an attitude of trying to do something that will gain the approval of others. The second stage leans towards abiding by the laws of the society in which a person lives and responding to the obligations of duty.

Kohlberg suggested that the third level is not reached by a majority of adults. The first stage is an understanding of social mutuality and genuine interest in the welfare of others. The second (and last) stage is based on respect for universal principles and demands of the individual conscience.

Kohlberg believed that moral development was sequential and individuals could not jump stages. He also suggested that if children were presented with moral dilemmas to discuss and talk through, their development to the next stage could be encouraged. He believed that moral development could be promoted through formal education, but at the same time recognised, as did Piaget, that much moral development comes about through social interactions.

Presenting and discussing moral dilemma's can encourage moral development

THINK IT OVER:

Watch a group of children playing a game with rules.

Ask yourself: are some of the children playing by the rules because they know that that is what is expected (the Conventional level of moral reasoning)?

Why do you think some of the children do not play by the rules?

The self-fulfilling prophecy

The way children see themselves in relation to other people around them influences how they behave and react. Children who are 'labelled' at an early age, for example, frequently being told that they are 'naughty', 'always in trouble', or 'very polite', may learn that this label is the way that they are expected to behave. This is often referred to as the **self-fulfilling prophecy**; in other words, label a child as naughty and that is the way they will behave.

CASE STUDY

There were four children, including a set of twins, in a family. The playgroup staff found it very difficult to manage the behaviour of the eldest boy and these difficulties continued throughout his school life. When child number two was old enough to attend playgroup, the staff made conscious efforts not to compare him to his brother, but also found his behaviour difficult to manage. By the time the second boy was in Year 2 at school, both boys had acquired a reputation for being difficult and their parents were frequent visitors to the school. Unfortunately, by the time the twins started playgroup the staff expected to have problems and they did. This was a self-fulfilling prophecy, almost as if staff had said to the children, 'Your brothers had behaviour problems, therefore you will too.'

1 How might the self-fulfilling prophecy have affected the children's self-concept?

2 What would you do in similar circumstances?

CHECKPOINT

1 Which theorists are usually associated with theories of social and emotional development?

2 What are the related elements of personality development according to Freud?

3 What could be a negative outcome, according to Erikson, of attempting to potty-train a child before they are physically capable of controlling their bladder and bowels?

4 What can influence your self-image?

5 Who developed the theory of attachment and how has this theory changed maternity practices?

6 What are the stages of separation?

7 According to Kohlberg, at about what age would you expect a child to behave according to socially-accepted norms because they are told to do so by an adult?

8 What is a self-fulfilling prophecy?

Chapter 4

How children's needs can affect behaviour

Introduction

As well as having an understanding of developmental theories and perspectives it is important that we also understand how children's needs can affect behaviour. Children's needs are expressed in different ways at different stages of their development. If we are to develop effective strategies for managing behaviour and empowering children, an understanding of needs and development is fundamental. This chapter is designed to help you gain greater understanding by focusing on:

◆ what children's needs are

◆ how needs and development are linked

◆ how needs can affect behaviour (the antecedents).

What are children's needs?

We all have needs that dominate our actions at different times in our lives. Physical or survival needs are often referred to as basic or physiological needs. Many theorists, such as **Abraham Maslow** (1908–1970) and **William Glasser** (born 1925), also suggest that we have psychological needs, such as to be loved, to belong, to have power and to have a sense of importance. Glasser suggests that these psychological needs must be met each day in order for each of us to be truly happy, human beings. If our needs are not met, for whatever reason, the consequences have an impact on every aspect of our development, including behaviour, and the ways we respond and react in given situations and to those around us.

Maslow's hierarchy of needs

Maslow is regarded by many as being one of the greatest thinkers of the twentieth century. He suggested that there are universal, instinct-like needs, which every human strives to satisfy. All human activity can be seen in terms of these needs. In 1962, Maslow produced a hierarchy of needs with those at the bottom of the hierarchy being essential to life. Maslow suggested that until the needs at one level of this hierarchy are met, individuals do not progress or move on to the next level.

SEEING THEORY IN PRACTICE

Many people think that basic or physiological needs are only relevant to babies and young children; however, this is not the case. Basic needs may become dominant at different times of our lives, depending on our circumstances and environment. A homeless adult has dominant needs that are concerned with their survival and so the needs associated with belonging are not necessarily a driving force. On the other hand, a young child in a nursery class may be more concerned with belonging to a peer group, rather than with when and where their next meal is coming from. It follows that psychological needs, as well as basic survival needs, have a considerable influence on children's development and are directly related to their behaviour.

Self-actualisation needs

Esteem needs

Belongingness and love needs

Safety needs

Physiological or basic needs

Maslow's hierarchy of needs

Self-actualisation needs: this can be described as the need to develop the individual's potential to the full, or 'reaching for dreams'. Early years workers can help children work towards this need by being enthusiastic and supportive towards them, perhaps by encouraging them to develop projects and plans, or by developing themselves. Individuals who are striving to meet self-actualisation needs are positive and optimistic about the future and they aim to promote these attitudes in others. They need to have others at the same level to interact with in order to meet their own needs.

Esteem needs: the need to have competence, the respect of others, self-confidence and pride. Early years workers can help children work towards this need by encouraging independence of thought and actions, offering and receiving praise when appropriate, showing respect for another's beliefs and belongings, being supportive and treating people with dignity.

Belongingness and love needs: in other words the need to feel accepted. Early years workers can help children meet this need by showing that they care, through listening attentively, being patient, showing respect for the child's family and encouraging interactions with others.

Safety needs: this is the need to be safe from harm. Early years workers can help children meet this need by knowing the procedures and policies, such as child protection, that will protect a child; they need to be alert to potential hazards and be able to identify risks and dangers by providing a safe environment. It is also important that adults caring for children maintain confidentiality in order to keep the child safe; know when and to whom they should report problems; and observe and record accurate information about the child.

Physiological or basic needs: these are the needs that must be met in order for anyone, child or adult, to survive. If these needs are not met, a child will not grow and develop. These needs are for food, fresh water, warmth, shelter and rest.

Some researchers have noted that Maslow's hierarchy follows the life cycle. A newborn baby's needs are almost entirely physiological. As the baby grows, it needs safety, then love. Toddlers are eager for social interaction. Teenagers are anxious about social needs. Young adults are concerned with esteem and it is often later in life that people transcend the first four levels to spend much time self-actualising, i.e. reaching their full potential in life.

On the other hand it can be shown that certain specific events and situations in an individual's life may mean that some needs will become more dominant than others, for example, the physiological needs of a homeless adult are more dominant than their need for esteem.

Maslow pointed out that the hierarchy is dynamic; the dominant need is always shifting. For example, a musician may be lost in the self-actualisation of playing music, but eventually becomes tired or hungry and so has to stop. Furthermore, a single action or behaviour may combine several levels; for example, eating a meal combines both physiological and social needs. The hierarchy does not exist by itself, but is affected by circumstances and the general culture. Satisfaction of a need is relative and, according to Maslow, a satisfied need no longer motivates. For example, a hungry child may be desperate for food, but once he or she eats a good meal, the promise of food no longer motivates their behaviour or actions.

Physiological or basic needs

Physiological or basic needs, such as air, water, nutrition, rest and shelter, are necessary for our survival. In order for children to develop in a healthy manner, these physiological or basic needs have to be met, as they are essential for normal growth. Indeed, if human beings are deprived of their basic needs, they place their own survival at risk. This can be seen all too graphically in countries where there is a shortage of food or clean water, or with elderly people who are unable to heat their homes adequately. Until basic needs are satisfied to the degree needed for the sufficient operation of the body, most of an individual's activity will be at this level and other needs will provide little motivation.

The spidergram below shows our basic physiological needs, and we will look at each of these in turn.

These basic needs must be met to ensure survival

Water

Water is essential for normal growth and development. Scientists have estimated that as much as 66 per cent of the human body weight is water. Small changes in the water levels in our cells can have very damaging effects on the body. Drinking dirty or contaminated water can also have serious effects on the body, as many diseases are water-borne. A need for water is indicated by thirst; if this need is not satisfied a person starts to feel excessively thirsty and activity is difficult. Active children and adults need frequent drinks of water throughout the day.

Food

Food is a complicated mixture of chemicals that supplies the body with energy and provides raw materials for growth and repair. The combination of food that we eat is called our diet and a healthy diet should contain a balance of carbohydrates, fats, proteins, vitamins, minerals, fibre and water. Some children, and adults, have specific conditions that restrict their diet, such as diabetes or coeliac disease. Children who have diabetes, for example, need to eat very regularly and avoid sugar. Some children react adversely to being given 'special' or different foods and so need to be handled with sensitivity and understanding. Food allergies are directly related to some behavioural conditions. Many foods are processed in some way before reaching our shops; the use of additives and colourings is widespread. These may have negative influences on a child's behaviour, as can be seen, for example, in the following case study.

SNAPSHOT

Mark was a five-year-old in a reception class who loved planning and constructing models. But his teacher noticed that after lunch he became very short-tempered, he would often hit out at children playing with him for no reason and on several occasions would scratch other children. When his teacher talked to Mark about why he did these things he said that he didn't know. Other children stopped playing with Mark and many were frightened of him. The teacher spoke to Mark's mother several times and neither of them could think of reasons why he behaved in this way. Mark's behaviour in nursery had not given any cause for concern. His mother was becoming increasingly upset and other parents were complaining to her about Mark's behaviour. The teacher had a yeast allergy and began to wonder if Mark also had a food allergy that might be affecting his behaviour. She suggested this to his mother who took Mark to see a nutritionalist. As Mark's behaviour was only unacceptable after lunch, the nutritionalist decided to investigate what he had eaten at lunch. Mark usually had sandwiches with a butter spread and either ham or cheese, a packet of crisps, a drink and a piece of fruit. Each day one item was left out of the lunch box and Mark's behaviour was closely watched. The teacher noticed that on the days the sandwiches or the crisps were omitted Mark was not quite so aggressive, so the link seemed to be in these foods. Mark's mother discovered that the same food colouring was present in the butter spread and crisps and so one day gave Mark sandwiches with no butter spread and no crisps. The results were dramatic: Mark went for a whole afternoon without hurting another child. Later tests by the nutritionalist showed that Mark was allergic to particular food colourings. Once this was established and they were removed from his diet, Mark's behaviour was not a problem at any time of the day.

The need for food is a physiological and basic need

Shelter and security

The need for shelter and security stays with us throughout our lives. Babies and young children have to depend on adults to fulfil this need and many adults rely on others to provide them with shelter. A lack of shelter or protection is a threat to our health and physical well-being. People who are homeless or those who are sleeping rough may show the visible effects of the lack of shelter. However, there are other adverse effects that are not visible. Homeless people, or those living in temporary accommodation, may feel very vulnerable, lack self-esteem and may also have feelings of very low self-worth.

The need to feel secure can also be linked to the need to form strong bonds and attachments as described in Chapter 3. Children who have not formed secure bonds may have difficulties with relationships and aspects of their emotional development.

Rest and sleep

The need for rest and sleep varies from person to person, but everyone needs a certain amount. Without adequate sleep and rest people may lack energy, become irritable, often fail to complete tasks, lose concentration and may become disorientated. A tired child is often fretful and unable to relate to others. Some children become aggressive or withdrawn. Children who do not have sufficient sleep over a period of time suffer physically; they may become more susceptible to infections and viruses, and they may have a poor appetite which in turn adversely affects their growth and development.

Fresh air

Fresh air may be almost a luxury in a busy town or city! However, being outside or in a well-ventilated room can prevent airborne bacteria and viruses entering the body. A stuffy room can cause headaches and a feeling of drowsiness. Being outside is often associated with vigorous play activities that often mean a person has to breathe deeply and exercise the whole body. Such forms of play allow children to develop co-ordination, learn to control large and small muscles and expend surplus energy. This last point is very important, as a child with lots of energy who spends periods of time physically inactive may become hyperactive and difficult to manage. Many childcare professionals and teachers will have dealt with a group of noisy hyperactive children who are full of energy due to the fact that they have not been able to go outside to play during the day because of the weather, and have been 'cooped up' in a stuffy classroom.

SNAPSHOT

In the past it was common practice for young babies to be put outside to sleep in prams regardless of the weather. It was believed that babies needed fresh air in order to develop. Fresh air was also regarded as essential for sick children. The former Agnes Hunt hospital near Oswestry in Shropshire cared for children with TB before and after the Second World War; one of its features was the open-air wards. This hospital no longer cares for children in this way, and now has modern hospital wards and children's areas specialising in orthopoedic care, but the walls of the corridors are lined with photographs from the 1950s.

The belief in the importance of fresh air that led to such practices is still strong in childcare today, but after some well-documented cases of babies in outside day-care arrangements dying, it is now believed that there are better ways of ensuring children have adequate fresh air.

Being free from infection and disease

People need to be protected from infection and disease, since frequent bouts of illness can hinder their development. For example, a child may become tired, withdrawn and disinterested in their surroundings. Good health practice, such as clean toilet facilities and encouraging children to wash their dirty hands, should minimise the threat of children coming in contact with infection and disease.

Exercise

Exercise and stimulation are essential to our overall development. In the early years, it is important to provide appropriate activities to stimulate a child. Children who lack opportunities to exercise become lethargic and may tire quickly. A lack of stimulating activities may sometimes lead to poor language and cognitive development, children may be slow to develop social skills and may have poor concentration.

It is important to remember that children with particular needs, such as those with limited mobility, need exercise and stimulation too. We should plan physical activities that are inclusive, such as activities on the floor to encourage rolling and movement, and passing and throwing games with balloons and balls.

SNAPSHOT

A recent report from Warwick University, as published in 'Nursery World' in April 2003, looked at case studies from educational and government-sponsored work in Britain. It reported that schools that place a greater emphasis on sport and physical activity have examples of remarkable improvements in behaviour across the whole school. It suggests that increasing the physical activity of children can lead to increased levels of concentration and increased self-esteem.

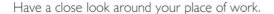

SEEING THEORY IN PRACTICE

Have a close look around your place of work.

Does the environment in which you work provide for your basic physiological needs, and those of the children?

Ask yourself the following questions:

◆ Is the room/building adequately heated and ventilated?

◆ Are there regular opportunities during the day for you and/or the children to visit the toilet, eat and drink?

◆ Do you feel safe and secure in the building or room?

◆ Is there an area where you or the children can rest if you need to?

◆ Is there somewhere where you and/or the children can wash and is that place clean and hygienic?

For each question that you answer with *No*, try to suggest ways that your needs could be met; for example, it might be a case of agreeing with others to open a window or door for part of the day, or turning down the central heating thermostat.

Safety and protection from stress

Once basic needs begin to be fulfilled, other levels of need become important and start to dominate the behaviour of an individual.

Safety needs and protection from stress take over in importance once physiological needs have been fulfilled. Safety needs are essentially the need to be free of the fear of physical danger and of the deprivation of basic needs. In other words, there is a need for self-preservation and a concern for the future. For adults this could involve being concerned about keeping their job so that they can provide food and shelter for the next day, week, or year. For children it could mean being reassured of their parents' presence to provide them with food, shelter and other basic needs, or trying to avoid being hurt or abused. If an individual's safety or security is in danger, other things seem unimportant.

Freedom from fear is very important for everyone; however, realistically it is not always possible for parents or adults working with children to eradicate all children's fears all of the time. Every child reacts differently to different situations and fears. It is important to remember that learning about fear is a normal part of growing up; for example, babies who show fear of strangers and become clingy with their primary carers are displaying common behaviour. Young children may have fears about things that do not exist, such as monsters under the bed or in the cupboard. Other children are simply afraid of the dark. However, these are normal feelings and it is important that adults treat these fears seriously. Often the more independent a child becomes, the greater the tendency to have fears. Fear is a natural response to events that are threatening to a child's personal security. Some fears are innate, i.e. they do not have to be learnt, such as the fear that is displayed by a baby when startled by a loud unseen noise or sudden movement. Some fears are learnt from others; for example, a child seeing an adult react in a scared and frightened way to a mouse or a spider will learn to be fearful of mice or spiders.

It is good practice to talk to children about their fears. This helps a child understand and deal with the emotions that they may be feeling and helps to develop relationships based on understanding and trust. Children need reassurance that their personal safety will not be threatened.

CASE STUDY

Read the following case study and then write down the sort of questions that Alice could ask her daughter to initiate a discussion about the fear of her mother not returning.

Alice left her daughter, Olivia, then aged two and a half, twice when she was suddenly hospitalised. On both occasions Olivia was cared for by her grandparents, but did not settle and repeatedly asked to see her mother. Unfortunately Olivia's father and grandparents decided that the sight of Mummy attached to tubes and machines would be too distressing for Olivia and so she did not visit the hospital. Eighteen months later Alice is convinced that Olivia still remembers being separated and believes that she doesn't trust her any more. Alice says that she can't go any where without taking Olivia and is becoming increasingly concerned about Olivia's reaction when she is left at nursery school. Alice makes a point of giving her daughter lots of cuddles and telling her how much she is loved, but Olivia is still convinced that her mother will go away one day and not return. Alice seeks advice from Olivia's teacher, Mrs Contreras, who suggests that it would be a good idea for mother and daughter to talk about Olivia's fears. She suggests that she should start by talking about things that Olivia likes to do and gradually lead into gentle questions about her fears. Mrs Contreras also suggests that Alice could talk to her daughter about significant events in the day such as break-time and lunch-time to help her understand at what point she will be returning, saying things such as, 'Mummy will come back to nursery after you have had a story with all of the other children.' The teacher advises that Olivia could be given something belonging to her mother to look after whilst she is at school as a form of security; this will help her to understand that her mother will come back. Alice should continue to cuddle her daughter at every opportunity and offer lots of reassurance.

ACTIVITY

Can you remember ever feeling anxious about something?

Did this feeling last a few moments, a few hours, a few days or much longer?

What did you do about it?

Make a chart like the example below and ask a close colleague or friend to do the same. Then compare your charts for similarities and differences.

Things that made me feel VERY anxious	How long it lasted	What I did	Things that made me feel A BIT anxious	How long it lasted	What I did
When I was little I was scared of dogs	Years	Avoided all dogs	Meeting a group of new people	About an hour	Took loads of deep breaths and talked positively to myself

Anxiety and stress can affect anyone at any time. Some people seem to thrive on living under pressure or stress, for example, taking on workloads that others might find too great. Stress and anxiety can make people physically ill, but at the same time it can be argued that no stress at all makes people very bored and possibly depressed – with nothing in their lives to get the adrenalin going! However, stress is not healthy if the need to feel safe and free of fear is not met.

THINK IT OVER:

Earlier in the chapter the importance of talking to children about their fears was emphasised. Look at the ways that you overcame your fears, in the Activity on page 47; how could you use these to help children?

There are several ways of helping children to talk about or overcome their fears. In the example given in the Activity, taking deep breaths was one coping technique – so encouraging children to think about their breathing can help them relax. Some children can be helped to relax by being with a caring adult in a calm and quiet environment, while others will begin to relax when spoken to in a calm and reassuring way. It is very important that carers acknowledge the child's feelings and are aware that their fears are genuine.

Older children can be encouraged to use a scale of 1 to 10 when talking about their fears, with 10 indicating a very severe fear. Younger children may respond better to pointing to pictures of faces showing degrees of fear to help express themselves and talk. For example:

Calm ⟶ Very scared

Younger children may be more able to relate to the idea of being filled up with fear, for example, up to their knees, or their waist, or all the way down to their finger tips, or completely full from their head to their toes.

Children can be introduced to the idea of 'positive' thoughts, for example, saying to themselves, 'I can do this, I can do this' or 'I will be fine, I will be fine'.

Children may experience anxiety and stress for many reasons. Some causes of stress are short-term, such as being left with another carer for a short time; other causes, for example, abuse, are long-term and have deep, long-lasting effects on a child's development and behaviour. Anxiety is usually associated with unpleasant emotional and physical feelings; only in the mildest short-term forms can we argue that some anxiety is necessary for normal development.

We all react in different ways to anxiety and stress. In general terms, children who are stressed or anxious may show changes in their behaviour. They may become disruptive, aggressive or clingy. They may revert to behaviours associated with younger children, such as needing a comforter or thumb-sucking. Some children who are anxious or stressed may masturbate frequently or for long periods of time. Sometimes there are clear physical signs such as loss of appetite, nausea or tension in the muscles that may make a child clumsy or lack co-ordination and control.

Freud

Freud suggested that individuals have a number of unconscious defence mechanisms which help to reduce anxiety. Defence mechanisms are mental processes which are instinctively activated when a state of anxiety occurs. Freud identified five main defence mechanisms:

1   **Repression** – when conflict happens between what we want and what we can have, we may become anxious. Freud believed that, as a result, whatever it is that we want will be repressed or pushed back into the unconscious to reduce the anxiety. For example, a child who is refused a biscuit will hopefully push the want to the 'back of their mind' instead of becoming stressful and anxious.

2   **Rationalising** – this is what we do when we do or think something that makes us feel a level of guilt – we might want to rationalise it to ourselves. For example, a child might say, 'It's not my fault, I thought that if I did . . .'.

3   **Projection** – if we cannot admit that we have certain feelings or patterns of behaviour, we might suppose that someone else has those feelings or behaviour patterns. For example, a child who has broken another child's toy might say, ' I didn't break it, someone else must have done it, and I don't tell lies.'

4   **Displacement** – we displace or transfer our own anxiety by blaming someone else for what we have done. For example, a person who has taken something in a shop without paying might say, 'Well they shouldn't leave things around and unattended, they're virtually making people steal.'

5   **Sublimation** – this is possibly a more successful defence mechanism whereby we focus our energies on something else which is more worthwhile. For example, a childcare worker might say to a child who is

frightened of meeting a dog on the way home, 'Let's not worry about that now, let's go and look at some books.'

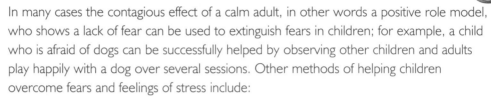

SEEING THEORY IN PRACTICE

In many cases the contagious effect of a calm adult, in other words a positive role model, who shows a lack of fear can be used to extinguish fears in children; for example, a child who is afraid of dogs can be successfully helped by observing other children and adults play happily with a dog over several sessions. Other methods of helping children overcome fears and feelings of stress include:

◆ talking, explanations and reassurance

◆ verbal explanations together with a practical demonstration that the feared object or situation is not dangerous

◆ giving a child examples of fearlessness regarding the feared object or situation

◆ conditioning the child to believe that the feared object is not dangerous but pleasurable. This can be done through role-play or, in non- threatening situations, playing with toys that resemble the feared object.

ACTIVITY

Consider the following scenarios and suggest possible ways of helping a child overcome their fear or feelings of stress:

◆ a child who has a fear of heights and has family friends and relatives who live in high-rise flats. The child becomes overwhelmed with anxiety when near a low railing or walking along a corridor

◆ a child who is frightened of spiders

◆ a child who is frightened of the dark.

Belongingness and love needs

Humans are social beings and have a need to belong to and to be accepted by various groups, such as their peers. When belongingness needs become dominant, individuals try their best to make meaningful associations with others. There is an enormous amount of evidence from the field of corporate management that providing an individual with a sense of belonging is fundamental in order for that person to excel. Many colleges, universities and other educational agencies publish mission statements to encourage positive values amongst their staff and adherents. For example, the Council for

Awards in Children's Care and Education (CACHE) mission statement reads:

'To raise the professional standards of children and young people's care and education, and to offer the best quality courses and qualifications as a service to children and their families.'

Belonging or having a social context is vital for the development of self-esteem and self-confidence. This is why Maslow put self-esteem above belonging in his hierarchy. Without a social framework in which to support an individual's perceived worth, self-worth is not *internalised* or personally taken in. This framework varies enormously, being small and tangible in the case of a baby, to being universal and highly abstract in the case of an artist.

From as early as three months old a baby reacts to the presence of a peer. Between six and nine months old a baby smiles directly at peers and may reach out and try to touch them. Children between two and four years old engage in simple turn-taking games with peers and show some level of co-operation. By the time a child is five years old peer groups are more important. Children of this age actively share activities with a common purpose or goal. Identity within the group becomes stronger as children have more and more worthwhile and satisfying interactions. Group identity becomes especially important when there is competition with other groups. Between the ages of ten and fourteen years, children may feel greater pressure to conform to the peer group, and often form intimate friendships.

It is a widely held belief that peer groups control the behaviour of children, sometimes more than parents or other adults. This control can be exerted in a variety of ways, from rewarding individuals who conform to the group's norms by inviting them to the 'right parties', or complimenting them on what they are wearing, to giving a child the 'silent treatment' and not talking to them, or bullying or ridiculing them.

Children need love and, like all human beings, need to know that they are loved, accepted and valued for the unique individuals that they are. This sounds straightforward enough, but many of the children who need love most are the ones who get it least. It is relatively easy for childcare workers and parents to love children who 'fit' their mental picture of the 'ideal' child, for example, clean, co-operative, bright, independent and developing 'normally'. But some people find it difficult to respond positively to children who do not fit their mental picture of the 'ideal' child – children who perhaps are demanding, unco-operative, exceptionally bright or developmentally delayed. These are situations when we really do need to think very carefully about our own views and values, as discussed in Chapter 1, and how they affect the way we behave towards children in particular.

THINK IT OVER:

Ryan is a six-year-old who is very demanding and constantly seeking attention. His teacher Julie admitted to feeling a sense of relief when Ryan caught chicken pox and didn't attend school for two weeks. Julie said,

> *'Although I was sorry that he was unwell, I was so relieved that I would not have to cope with his constant questioning and attention-seeking behaviour. I could spend more time with the other children, knowing that we would not be interrupted by Ryan.'*

Be really honest and ask yourself whether you have ever felt a feeling of relief when you were told that a particular child would not be attending school or nursery. Do you think that the child knows that you feel this way?

The chances are that the child *is* aware and this can encourage them to continue being demanding because they will get negative attention – which is better than no attention at all.

> *The feeling of belonging … contributes to the inner well being, security and identity. Children need to know that they are accepted for who they are. They should know that what they can do can make a difference and that they can explore and try out new activities.*

> New Zealand Ministry of Education (1996)

If all children are to be reached, then the adults who work with them and care for them must create a sense of belonging for children and find ways of letting them know that they are loved – no matter what. Part of creating a sense of belonging is showing that we care; this can be done in a variety of ways. Telling a child that we care is a positive start, but there is the danger as with many things that when the same words or phrases are repeatedly used that they lose their impact; for example, the adult who always says, 'That's nice', to a child regardless of whether they are looking at a painting, listening to a child talk about an event or commenting on an action of the child, will find that their words become ineffective as the child ignores the comment.

We can tell a child that we care by using a range of different words and phrases, and by using body language, gestures and facial expressions, such as spontaneous smiles. We can let a child know that we care by listening attentively to what they are saying, by giving them our full attention, by making eye contact and by giving appropriate responses and asking questions. Making a child feel accepted in a situation also shows that we care and helps meet the need for belonging; for example, making sure that every child has a special role or job to do during tidy-up time, so that no one is left out of activities, unless they specifically don't want to join in. Many children are helped by knowing and understanding the routine of the day or session as this gives them a structure and security. This can help them to anticipate what is going to happen and has the added security factor of making them feel comfortable and accepted.

Self-esteem – how we see ourselves

Once individuals begin to satisfy their need to belong, they generally want to be more than just a member of a group. They then feel the need for esteem – both self-esteem and recognition from others. **Jillian Rodd** (1996), writing in *Understanding Young Children's Behaviour* (Allen and Unwin), states that there are three facets to self-esteem, as can be seen in the diagram below.

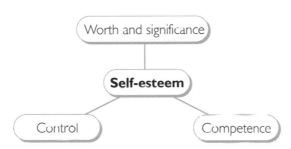

There are three essential elements of self-esteem

1   **Worth and significance** – children need to feel accepted, loved and respected by those around them; in other words, they need to meet the needs of the third level of Maslow's hierarchy. Without these feelings of worth and significance children develop low or poor self-esteem, because it is very difficult for them to feel good about themselves if they know that they are unloved and rejected by others.

2   **Competence** – children need to feel competent and capable. This will encourage them to learn new skills, feel motivated and become increasingly autonomous. Obviously competence is limited by a child's age, size and stage of growth and development, but it may also be affected by unrealistic expectations of what a child can achieve. Repeated failure can lead to frustration and dissatisfaction. Consequently a child will develop negative views of their own competences and have low self-esteem.

3   **Control** – the level of an individual's self-esteem may be directly affected by the amount of control he or she feels that they have over a situation or their environment. Even young children can gain control over their environment, for example, when a baby cries and his or her parent or carer comes to find out why. Children quickly learn that when they behave in a certain way, their actions can produce a change in their environment.

Esteem needs

Maslow divided esteem needs into two groups:

◆ internal needs such as self-respect, autonomy and achievement

◆ external needs such as status recognition and attention.

Most people have a need for a high evaluation of themselves that is firmly based in reality – recognition and respect from others. Satisfaction of these needs produces feelings of self-confidence, prestige, power and control. People begin to feel that they are useful and have some effect on their environment; these individuals could be described as having high self-esteem. Individuals who regard themselves in a negative way are described as having low or poor self-esteem.

There are occasions when children are unable to satisfy their need for esteem through appropriate and constructive behaviour. When this is the case a child may resort to disruptive or inappropriate behaviour; they may, for example, throw a 'temper tantrum', in the same way (and for the same reasons) that adults might start an argument with people at work. Consequently, through disruptive or inappropriate behaviour a child may gain the recognition they have failed to achieve through constructive or appropriate behaviour. In fact, it could be argued that some of the social problems in today's society have their origin in esteem needs not being met.

CASE STUDY

Read through the following scenario and then answer the questions.

Kirsty maintains that she wants the best for Callum, her three-year-old son, and makes sure that he has every opportunity to 'do well'. Callum is bright and keen to learn new things. Kirsty and other members of Callum's family often tell him that he is a 'clever boy'. Kirsty has bought several books to help Callum learn to read, as she believes that if he can read by the time he starts school he will have a head start. At first Callum sat quietly whilst Kirsty went through some of the activities in the books with him and he quickly began to recognise the letters of his name. After a while, Callum wouldn't respond to Kirsty's questions and eventually began to have temper tantrums whenever she produced the books. Kirsty became cross with Callum and one day shouted at him that she was fed up with him and he was a very naughty boy.

1 Suggest some reasons why Callum stopped responding.

2 What are the possible effects on Callum?

3 What do you think Kirsty should do?

4 Is this an appropriate activity for a three-year-old? Can you think of more appropriate play activities for Kirsty and Callum, such as playing with small-scale toys to develop his vocabulary?

Self-actualisation needs

Once the need for self-esteem has been largely met Maslow stated, 'we will develop a new restlessness and the urge to pursue the unique gifts or talents that may be particular to that person.' Maslow referred to this final level of need as 'self-actualisation'. It is suggested by many psychologists that only people in a later stage of life will rise above the first four levels of Maslow's hierarchy to spend time self-actualising. However, this does not necessarily mean that children will not feel a need to achieve this level. Self-actualisation is concerned with meeting one's potential. It includes self-expression and creativity as much as the need to search for identity and the meaning of life. If this need is not met, a child could feel restless and bored and lack a zest for life. On the other hand, if this need *is* met children can be creative, positive, energetic, curious and open to new experiences and ideas.

It is important to remember that Maslow's hierarchy does not necessarily always follow the pattern described in the previous sections. Maslow did not intend the hierarchy to be applied wholesale. He felt that the hierarchy was a typical pattern that works most of the time. He accepted, however, that there were numerous exceptions to this generalisation. For example, the Indian leader Mahatma Gandhi frequently sacrificed his physiological and safety needs for the satisfaction of other needs when India was striving for independence from Britain. In his historic fasts, Gandhi went for weeks without nourishment to protest about governmental injustices. He was operating at the self-actualisation level whilst some of his other needs were unsatisfied.

THINK IT OVER:

The structure of our schools and the curricula are based on the assumption that most children who come into school have had their physiological and safety needs met at home. There are now practices and policies in place to support physiological needs, such as breakfast clubs and subsidised meals, and safety needs, such as road safety, sex, drug and health education in many schools, but this does not alter the fact that children upon entering school are immediately expected to learn. Success in academic school work is expected to foster the children's sense of self-worth, which will in turn enable them to join the community and society as 'responsible individuals'. It could be argued that children are now required, almost, to *learn* their right to belong.

Linking needs and development

It is widely accepted that growth and development can be loosely divided in the following way:

◆ physical and sensory development

◆ cognitive and language development

◆ social and emotional development.

The links between development and needs are numerous. Some are very obvious, for example, the need for food has to be met in order for children to grow physically. Some are less obvious, such as the need for self-actualisation and emotional development. Meeting a child's needs in terms of development is not only about keeping a risk-free and hygienic environment or providing stimulating activities or a balanced diet. Some of the links are explained in the following sections, some are not; it is up to you to determine where a link can be made and when to trust your own professional judgement.

Physical and sensory development

Physical development can be defined as the process of maturing and growth through which children gain control of their bodies and their movements. Most children have acquired all the basic skills concerned with control and movement by the time that they are six or seven, and although they continue to grow and develop they are, in fact, building on and refining their basic skills.

Physiological needs, that is, bodily needs such as food and water, are placed first in Maslow's hierarchy , because they tend to dominate until they are satisfied. When these basic needs are met the body is able to operate effectively, fight infection, develop and refine skills, grow and mature. It is also important to remember that physical development can be affected by other needs. For example, a child who lives in fear, physical danger or deprivation also fails to thrive physically.

Sensory development is an important aspect of physical development. Sight, hearing, smell, touch and taste all depend on the appropriate organs and nerves developing and maturing. A child whose basic physiological needs are not met may not only be slow to grow and develop in size, height and weight, but may also have sensory impairments, for example, a deterioration in their eyesight due to a lack of nourishment, vitamins and nutrients.

A child who is undernourished and lacking in food, fails to thrive physically, but other areas of their development are also affected. For example, lack of energy caused by poor nourishment may prevent children from exploring; they may feel listless and tired, and not be motivated to learn and find out new things.

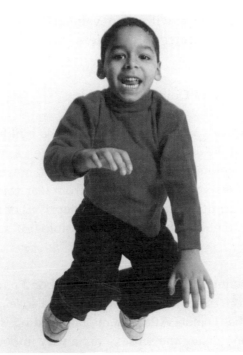

By the time most children are 6 they have control of their movements e.g. jumping

They may have poor levels of concentration. A child who is fighting an infection may not want to play and socialise, but may need to sleep more than normal and possibly be less hungry.

Sensory development is also an important aspect of cognitive development. Piaget named the first stage of his theory of cognitive development the **sensori-motor stage** as children use their senses to provide information for the brain. Babies and young children explore and learn about their environment through their senses. Babies put many objects in their mouths in order to explore shape, feel and texture, as the mouth is very sensitive and can send innumerable messages to the brain about the object being examined. Many young children have to hold something in their hands, in order to 'see' it properly, the sense of touch being an important way to send information to the brain.

Sensory information that is sent to the brain helps children stay attentive and to concentrate. Multi-sensory activities, those in which children can use sight, touch, smell, hearing and touch, can be very effective in helping children develop concentration skills and learn how to differentiate between experiences. A meal with others, for example, can be a valuable multi-sensory experience for all children.

Cognitive (intellectual) and language development

Cognitive development is about how children learn, how thought processes develop and how those thoughts and knowledge are organised. How children learn is a matter of constant debate with many valid and relevant theories (see Chapter 2). A simple way to consider how children learn might be to think about MUD:

Memory, **U**nderstanding and **D**oing

Memory is the ability to recall specific information and so build on and learn from experiences. Look again at the case study of Katy on page 14 in Chapter 2. Katy used her memory to change the pattern of her behaviour; however, it could be argued that Katy's need for security and freedom from fear was not being met as she was being bullied. In addition Katy was being deprived of food (although for a relatively short period), therefore Katy's basic physiological needs were not being met either.

A baby uses his or her memory of smells to allow it to bond effectively with a main carer or parent. It recognises the carer by smell and so learns to respond to and communicate with that person. Attachment and bonding whilst employing aspects of physical development – the senses – are a very important part of emotional and social development.

All of us store in our memories experiences that we may not need to use immediately. These memories surface at a later date, to be used and possibly modified. It is generally accepted that people tend to remember things that are important, but to forget less significant things, for example, we might easily remember where and what time to meet a friend that we haven't seen for a while, but forget which level of the car park we left our car!

Another aspect of memory is **perception**, or how we differentiate and take in images and experiences. Perception is often closely linked to sensory development as we use the information from our senses to enable us to build up a picture or an image. Perception can be defined as the process of organising and interpreting sensory information. The old story of a group of blind men feeling an elephant shows this clearly as they each declare the elephant to be something different, such as a tree or a snake, using information based on the sensory experiences stored in their memories. In order to develop perception a baby needs sensory stimulation. Many parents report that their young babies gaze intently at their faces; this allows the baby to absorb visual information about the parent and so develop and organise a mental image. As children grow and develop, their perception relies not only on sensory information but also on the ability to be attentive; for example, a young child learning to read needs to acquire different kinds of visual discrimination from those they have used for differentiating between different people. They must begin to pay attention to similarities and variations of letter shapes, as well as aspects of their visual environment that they may have ignored before. Consider, for example, the visual differences between the letters **c**, **e** and **o**; they are only very minor differences, as are those between the words **cot** and **cat**.

Understanding is an active process, involving thoughts which link or group together in a new way. To help understand new ideas we must find out about the subject in a way that makes sense to us. This means asking questions, making comparisons and solving problems. Asking questions involves language and communication in some form; it also involves using memory to recall information that is already understood. Many would argue that the development of language is also a physical skill as the musculature development and breathing control required to make intelligible sounds are aspects of physical development. As discussed before, physical development is affected if physiological needs are not met.

Any form of communication is a two-way process with a giver and receiver. Therefore a child needs to have established meaningful relationships with others in order to communicate effectively. This is the third level of Maslow's hierarchy of needs.

Doing involves learning through first-hand experiences, from actions, from exploring the environment and through play. Piaget concluded that children learn from their actions and from actively exploring their environment through their senses. As before, if physiological needs are not met, sensory development will be impaired and this will affect learning. Learning by doing normally involves some understanding of what is to be achieved, or a purpose or motivation. Maslow's hierarchy is frequently referred to as a theory of motivation, in that the fulfilment of one level of needs motivates the individual to try to fulfil those of the next level. Young children are often motivated to do something out of inquisitiveness and a general desire to find out more about their environment. It is therefore very important that the environment that they explore is safe and secure and that they feel safe and free from fear.

Children need to be alert and attentive if they are going to be able to make sense of the information that their brains receive. It may be that in order to make sense and use certain pieces of information they have to focus on one particular thing, such as the shape of letters. Most children are able to do this as they grow and develop, but some, such as those who have been identified with Attention Deficit Hyperactivity Disorder (ADHD), will find this more difficult. This will affect how they react and behave. Using props or visual aids and memory prompts is an effective way of helping children focus and concentrate.

THINK IT OVER:

Imagine that you want to learn to cook a completely new recipe that you have found in a book. What would be the most effective way for you to learn?

1 You could read the book and then rely on your *memory* to collect all the right ingredients, remember the order for adding them and cooking times and so on.

2 You could read the book and use your previous knowledge of cookery to help you *understand* what is required.

3 You could go to a demonstration and watch someone else cooking.

4 You could have the book in front of you and actually *do* it yourself at a time of day when you are feeling hungry, and then eat the meal.

ACTIVITY

Think of something in your own life that you have learnt by doing, such as learning to drive a car, mixing up formula feeds, or embroidery. Write down the process that you went through in order to learn to do this.

◆ What was the most significant factor that helped you to learn?

◆ Can you relate this factor to Maslow's hierarchy of needs?

Social and emotional development

Social and emotional development is very closely linked to all other areas of development. For example, a child who is delayed in their language development as a result of a physical impairment, may find it difficult to communicate with others, which in turn may affect their ability to socialise and form relationships. The child may feel insecure and frustrated at their level of skill, and this in turn may show in the way the child behaves in certain situations.

The theories of both Piaget and Kohlberg show that young children do not usually have a concept of right and wrong, and often behave in unacceptable ways to avoid punishment. In fact, very young children do not understand many social concepts, such as sharing or playing a game according to rules, and so do not understand why they cannot have everything that they can see that is within their grasp. This is especially true when behaviour is dominated by basic physiological needs; for example, when a child 'needs' or wants a biscuit and the adult refuses, the child is frustrated and becomes angry.

SNAPSHOT

A play worker in an after-school club said that he spends much of his time developing relationships with the children whilst playing alongside them. Colin said '*I firmly believe that children need to feel secure in their relationships with the adults and other children. I spend much of my time talking with children about their feelings. We talk all the time. It is one of the most effective ways that I know to build self-esteem, and confidence and to promote positive behaviour within the club.*' Colin went on to talk about Scott, who came to the club each day. Scott had few friends and other children complained that he disrupted their play. Colin said that at first Scott was very reluctant to talk to him, but eventually he told Colin that he was '*rubbish and always in trouble at school*'. The play workers always greeted each child individually and made certain that they added a comment such as 'good to see you' each time Scott arrived. Colin took every opportunity to talk to Scott about what he was doing, how he felt that day, just about anything. Colin admitted that there weren't changes overnight, and sometimes it was difficult to get Scott to talk, but gradually Scott's self-esteem and confidence did improve and he is now taking an active part in the club forum and is in his school's football team.

CHECKPOINT

1 Briefly explain why some researchers believe that Maslow's hierarchy of needs follows the life cycle.

2 In terms of emotional development, babies and young children are very dependent on their main carers. How does this link to Maslow's hierarchy of needs?

3 How can a lack of water affect a child's behaviour?

4 Freud suggested that we have five defence mechanisms to help us reduce anxiety. What are they?

5 What, according to Maslow, are internal needs?

6 According to Maslow, under what circumstances might a person start an argument with a colleague, or might a child have a 'temper tantrum'?

7 How do breakfast clubs support Maslow's theory?

8 How might lack of nourishment affect a child's behaviour?

9 Piaget advocated 'active play'. How does this link to a child's needs?

10 Explain why a young child may become frustrated and angry when refused a biscuit?

Chapter 5

The legal framework for current practice

Introduction

In historical terms, the concepts of empowering children and managing behaviour are relatively new ideas. For centuries the idea of 'childhood' did not exist and, as many historical paintings show us, children were regarded as smaller versions of adults. This chapter considers how ideas and views of behaviour have changed over the centuries and how legislation affecting children has developed up to the present time. The chapter will look at:

- ◆ the historical background to the current legal framework
- ◆ current legislation
- ◆ ways that the legal framework impacts on our practice.

The historical background to the current legal framework

Before the twentieth century

The image of childhood that we have is so familiar to us that it is easy to assume it is a universal concept, one that has always existed historically and one that cuts across geographical and social divisions. However, some theorists, such as Philippe Aries in *Centuries of Childhood: A Social History of Family Life* (1962), argue that the state of childhood is a product of modern Western society and that this concept did not exist in the pre-modern age. Historically children were regarded as different from adults only in that they were smaller. Children were dressed in

The Blue Boy by Thomas Gainsborough

smaller versions of adults' clothes, worked alongside adults and effectively belonged to an adult society. This view is clearly shown in paintings such as 'Kinderspiele' by Pieter Bruegel the Elder (1525–1569), 'Las Meninas', by Diego Rodriguez de Silva y Velázquez (1599–1660) and 'The Blue Boy' by Gainsborough (1727–1788). All of these famous paintings depict children dressed in the same style of clothes as adults and in adult poses. However, this idea does not suggest that children were neglected or not loved, but that as soon as they could live without the constant attention of their mother, nanny or cradle-rocker, they could take their place in adult society.

Historically, the provision of an education for children was not seen as of benefit to the child, but more as a means of providing the skills to enable the future adult to take their place in society. But education was not available to all. Schools such as Eton, founded in 1440, taught classical languages and religion to the sons of the wealthy. Misdemeanours were dealt with harshly, beatings, humiliation and deprivation being common forms of punishment. William Shenstone's poem 'The School Mistress' written in 1742, says:

> *'A matron old, whom we Schoolmistress name*
> *Who boasts unruly brats with birch to tame'*

Children who were considered to behave in anti-social ways, such as those who stole, were dealt with under the same laws at adults. Children could be imprisoned, sentenced to death or transported to penal colonies such as Botany

Bay in Australia. *Oliver Twist*, written in 1837–9 by Charles Dickens, gives us a very graphic image of how children could be treated by society.

THINK IT OVER:

In the past children were dressed like adults, were regarded as miniature versions of adults and their behaviour and actions were judged by 'adult' criteria.

Think again about your own values and views, as discussed in Chapter 1.

Do you think that history has influenced current thinking about empowerment and guiding children to manage their own behaviour?

The British philosopher John Locke (1632–1704) believed that every child was born as a 'blank slate', which meant that they were neither innately good, nor innately bad. It was up to adults to teach children through rewards and punishments, modelling and association. This view in many ways perpetuated the belief that children needed to be controlled by adults. It resulted in many philanthropic and often religious individuals taking it upon themselves to 'save' children from what they believed were situations where they could be corrupted, such as mines and factories. Many children who were 'saved' from mines or factories were left with nothing to occupy their days and no means of income. By the beginning of the 1800s this had become a major problem in industrial areas for large numbers of children. One way of tackling this problem was instigated by the Society for Investigating the Causes of the Alarming Increase of Juvenile Delinquency in the Metropolis, in 1815. This resulted in formal structures to control under-occupied children by placing them in either reformatory institutions or industrial schools. Later, Factory Acts were established to restrict the length of time children could be employed and to set precedents for school attendance. The **Education Act (1870)** introduced the concept of compulsory schooling between the ages of five and ten. Schools established around this time often had large classes, encouraged mechanical rote-learning and enforced strict, authoritarian discipline.

Historically, the development of legislation and the change in society's views of children and childhood have done little to empower children; rather they have replaced one set of limitations with another.

THINK IT OVER:

Sayings such as *'children should be seen but not heard'* and *'spare the rod and spoil the child'* indicate how some people used to regard children. Do you think these sayings still reflect the views of some people today?

After 1900 and up to the present day

Education Act (1902)

This act attempted to formalise the provision of education in Britain and the training of teachers. It was rapidly followed in 1904 by the **Elementary School Code,** which showed a new and official view of education. This code stated that:

> *The purpose of the elementary public school is to form and strengthen the character and to develop the intelligence of the children entrusted to it.*
> © *Crown copyright*

Discipline was still harsh and strictly enforced and the practice of sending children under the age of fourteen to prison was not abolished until the **Children Act (1908)**.

SNAPSHOT

Mrs Marjorie Evans, now in her eighties, attended a large school in Manchester in the 1920s. She recalls up to sixty children between the ages of five and seven in her class, with the girls sitting in rows on one side of the room and the boys on the other. She remembers being very afraid of the teacher, and that no child dared to speak out of turn or do anything which could have been called 'misbehaving', for fear of being caned. The teacher maintained this discipline by shouting at children and caning them.

Eglantyne Jebb (1876–1928), who founded Save the Children in 1919, was a great exponent of children's rights and worked tirelessly for universal recognition of these rights. In 1923 she summarised for the first time in a document some of the essential rights of children, and these became the Declaration of the Rights of the Child. This declaration was agreed by the General Assembly of the International Save the Children Union in 1923. A year later the declaration was adopted by the League of Nations and became known as the **Declaration of Geneva**. However, this declaration was not given the legally binding status that could have forced governments to enshrine it in law. Still, it represented a movement in attitudes towards children.

Subsequent **Education Acts** in **1936** and **1944** were mainly concerned with the administration of education rather than its content. Neither act considered children's rights or gave guidelines for disciplinary procedures. However, both these acts were produced during a time of significant change – the Second World War.

The Plowden Report (1967)

We must remember that reports are not pieces of legislation, but they do often lead to acts. The Plowden Report was an important document in the active debate on child-centred education, and although it has now become 'unfashionable', it was perhaps the first official document to acknowledge the rights of children since 1924, especially in allowing them to follow their own interests in the classroom. Many feared that these ideas would lead to a lack of teacher control and children 'just doing what they wanted'. In many ways the Plowden Report sowed the seeds of empowerment, and was the turning point for current legislation.

Current legislation

There is not sufficient scope here to discuss in detail the content of the many pieces of current legislation affecting children's education. However, reading the texts of key documents is important and rewarding for people working in childcare. If you do not have copies of the documents to refer to, see page 213 for addresses from which to obtain them.

The table below summarises what the key items of current legislation say.

Legislation	Focus of legislation
Education Act (1981)	First official recognition of: • Special educational needs (leading on from the **Warnock Report (1978)**) • Parents' rights regarding children's education.
Education Reform Act (1988)	National Curriculum introduced into schools. (Debate and anxiety among educational professionals: is this government placing inappropriate constraints on children, teachers and schools?)
UN Convention on the Rights of the Child (1989)	A formal statement agreed by many nations, stating that every child (age 0–18 years) has a right to: • good food • education • shelter • play • being able to say what they think and be listened to • protection from abuse. Main points of the Convention: • Article 2: All rights apply to children whatever their background, and the state has an obligation to protect children against discrimination. • Article 3: Children's best interests must come first. • Article 12: Children have a right to be heard, and they have a right to express their views in all matters affecting them. • Article 19: Children must be protected from violence, neglect and abuse. • Article 23: Children with disabilities and learning difficulties must have their rights protected.
Children Act (1989)	First acknowledgement in UK law of children's rights, encapsulated by the phrase 'the needs of the children are paramount'. States rights of a child to basic standards of care, nurture and upbringing. Sets out rights and responsibilities of all people legally caring for children.

Legislation	Focus of legislation
Education Act (1993)	Made two key proposals: • Secretary of State required to publish a Code of Practice for children with special educational needs (see below). • Parents of children under the age of two years have the right to ask for their children to be formally assessed – the aim being to identify and meet the needs of the child earlier and more effectively.
Education Act (1996)	All acts since 1944 incorporated into one. A time frame set on the legal process for identifying and assessing a child's needs as set out in the Code of Practice.
Human Rights Act (1998)	Became legal in 2000, the result of requirements laid down by the European Convention on Human Rights. All government policy and judgements must be made in accordance with the articles of this act. Includes the Right to Education (Article 2 of Protocol 1), curbing the power of schools to exclude children.
Code of Practice for the Identification and Assessment of Children with Special Educational Needs (1994, revised 2001)	Practical guidance to local education authorities and governing bodies of all schools in receipt of public funding on their responsibilities towards children with special educational needs. Important examples of the recommended good practice. • Children with behavioural and emotional difficulties should be assessed and appropriate provision and support instigated. • Children with special educational needs should be educated together with their peers – the 'inclusive' approach.
National Standards for Under Eights Day Care and Childminding (2001)	Early years providers must meet a set of 14 standards. These include: • Standard 9: Adults must actively promote equality of opportunity and anti-discriminatory practice for all children in their care. • Standard 10: Adults must be aware that some children in their care have special needs, and they must take steps to promote the welfare and development of such children. • Standard 11: Adults caring for children must be able to manage a wide range of children's behaviour in a way that promotes their welfare and development.
Birth to Three Matters – a Framework of Effective Practice (2002)	Not strictly legislation, but aims to support, inform, guide and challenge early years practitioners. Complements the National Standards (see above) and also the Curriculum Guidance for the Foundation Stage (DfES/QCA, 2000). Focuses on the child, moving away from traditional subjects/areas of experience/curriculum headings. It considers four aspects: • A strong child • A skilful communicator • A competent learner • A healthy child. A milestone in recognising and valuing babies and young children, and giving status to those who work within this age group.

Ways that the legal framework impacts on our practice

Educational legislation over the years has had a great impact on the practice of childcare. Now, when adults or organisations make decisions that affect children, for example, when forming policies and setting up procedures, they must always think first about what would be best for the children, how their needs can be met fairly and, in doing so, uphold the law. For example, as a result of the influence on law and public policy of the UN Convention on the Rights of the Child, it has followed that children in nurseries, schools and other settings are able to express their views about the services they attend and to influence those services and their experience of them. Huge importance has been placed on listening to children. In the UK there are moves to consult more widely with children, with the introduction of forums and school councils, although this does not include the rights of children in early years settings. All children are now considered to have the right to have choices and independence within the boundaries of safe practices.

THINK IT OVER:

1 Do early years workers listen to and act upon the views of children in their care, particularly in relation to behaviour management strategies?

2 How can an early years worker allow children to have choices and be independent whilst at the same time preventing them from hurting one another or damaging the property of another individual?

The Children Act (1989) is one piece of UK legislation that has had far-reaching implications for all who work with and care for children. For example, the act has placed much responsibility on local authorities to meet basic childcare requirements, particularly when parents are unable to meet their child's right to basic standards of care and nurture. In child abuse cases the local authority may need to work with the families to prevent further abuse, or, in particularly serious instances, is now empowered to remove a child from their family altogether. The Thomas Coram Research Unit at the Institute of Education, University of London, produced an interim report in 1994 of a study on the implementation of the Children Act as it affected day care and educational provision for children under eight years across Britain. The unit found that more emphasis was being placed on a multi-agency approach (especially in Wales), and it had been recognised that restructuring in local authorities was required. We have now seen Early Years Development and Childcare Partnerships established across the country and initiatives, such as Sure Start, gaining momentum and having an impact.

Corporal punishment

An example of the impact of the legal framework on childcare practice is the ongoing controversy about child smacking. In a sense, the first part of the argument has been won as a direct result of legislation: the Children Act demanded that childcare settings should have proper behaviour management policies based on 'positive' strategies, and in most settings 'corporal punishment (smacking, slapping or shaking) should not be used'. Now, in most childcare and educational settings, physical, or corporal, punishment is illegal. At the present time, only childminders, with written permission from a child's parents, can legally smack a child. However, a childminder who is a member of the National Childminding Association will, by becoming a member, automatically give up the right to smack a child. It is also worth remembering that it is now a legal minefield for a person who wants to use physical punishment to manage children's behaviour – such incidents can lead to accusations of abuse.

The arguments against smacking

The second stage in the argument about child smacking continues: should *anybody*, even a parent or primary carer, be allowed to smack a child in their care? The argument revolves around such issues as: what constitutes a smack? What might be a light smack to one individual could be a hard slap to another. A related problem is: where should a slap be administered? On the hand, the back of the leg, across the buttocks?

Many people believe that giving a child a smack is a quick, instant and effective way of stopping a child behaving in a certain way; for example, smacking a child immediately after they have thrown a toy and broken something. On the other hand, it could be argued that a smack is a negative reinforcer (see Chapter 2 for theories of behaviour). A short sharp negative reinforcer was one of the methods of modifying the behaviour of rats in B. F. Skinner's experiment, although the rats were not smacked but given an electric shock. Verbal disapproval and raised voices may often be associated with smacking. This, combined with the physical pain, may make a child very frightened and they may learn not to repeat an action due to fear, rather than understanding why the action was not approved by the adult.

It is in itself an indication of the impact of changing childcare practices that the issue continues to be debated – attitudes are gradually changing. The legal and moral arguments against any form of child smacking are mounting. Many European countries, such as Sweden, have legislation which makes it a criminal offence to smack children.

> Smacking is considered a form of abuse. These strategies have no place in childcare and educational settings; and early years professionals should use positive methods to manage children's behaviour.

Research in several countries has shown that children should not be subjected to any form of physical abuse:

First, there is a moral issue. Is it right for one person to be violent towards another? If an adult hits another adult, they are committing a criminal offence but in Britain if an adult hits a child, they are not technically breaking the law, although the adult might be charged with abuse. The adult is physically much bigger than the child and is therefore in a more powerful position. The message that may be given to the child is that it is acceptable for powerful and bigger people to hit smaller less powerful individuals.

Smacking can teach a child that it is acceptable to be aggressive. Smacking is a form of anger, an aggressive response to an action. In such situations it could be argued that the person who is doing the smacking is not in full control of their feelings. Children learn from role models and so they may not learn to control their own anger in non-violent or aggressive ways, if they see adults smacking. In some cases physical punishments injure children, and in extreme cases cause fatalities.

Smacking does not teach children how to resolve problems or conflicts in a peaceful way. Smacks are often delivered immediately after the misdemeanour has occurred and often with no chance for either the child or adult to explain their actions. Frequently, individuals who smack are not consistent about when or why they deliver the smack. This can confuse children and so they are not able to learn acceptable boundaries for their behaviour. People sometimes criticise other sectors

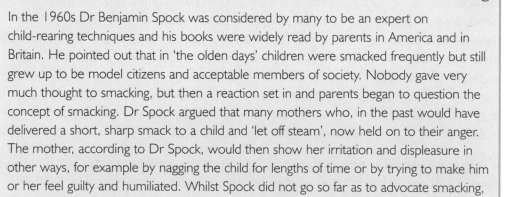

THINK IT OVER:

In the 1960s Dr Benjamin Spock was considered by many to be an expert on child-rearing techniques and his books were widely read by parents in America and in Britain. He pointed out that in 'the olden days' children were smacked frequently but still grew up to be model citizens and acceptable members of society. Nobody gave very much thought to smacking, but then a reaction set in and parents began to question the concept of smacking. Dr Spock argued that many mothers who, in the past would have delivered a short, sharp smack to a child and 'let off steam', now held on to their anger. The mother, according to Dr Spock, would then show her irritation and displeasure in other ways, for example by nagging the child for lengths of time or by trying to make him or her feel guilty and humiliated. Whilst Spock did not go so far as to advocate smacking, he thought that it was less harmful to children than lengthy and protracted disapproval because it cleared the air quickly for both the child and the parent.

1 What do you think?

2 Was Dr Spock right in his argument that it is better to let go of strong emotions and clear the air quickly?

3 If you are a parent, what do you do?

of society for violent acts, such as during demonstrations that were intended to be peaceful events, but those same people might use physical punishment on their children without realising that they are condoning violent behaviour.

Many young children do not understand the reasons why they have been smacked. This lack of understanding does not enable children to learn acceptable boundaries for their behaviour and, in some cases, the fear of being smacked and physically hurt is so great that children may tell lies about what they have been doing. Extensive research has shown that physical punishment is not an effective way to manage children's behaviour. Positive management strategies such as praise and rewards have proved to be more effective.

Committee of Rights Report

There are limits, however, to how far legislation is allowed to affect childcare practices. In October 2002 the United Nations urged the British government to change the law that currently allows parents to smack their children. The Committee of Rights Report (2002) on the United Kingdom's record of protecting children said that the government should outlaw all corporal punishment in the family. The report also regretted the defence of 'reasonable chastisement' allowed by the government despite recommendations. The government responded that it promoted positive, participative and non-violent forms of discipline. However, following this report a national television company asked viewers to take part in a telephone vote as to whether parents should be allowed to smack their children. The result was overwhelmingly in favour of smacking, with 65 per cent of the vote stating that parents should be allowed to smack their children. Clearly, the childcare practices of ordinary people impact on legislation, and there is some way to go in changing attitudes before legislation is allowed to move this argument forward.

CHECKPOINT

1 Historically, what was the view of 'childhood'?

2 What was one of the main impacts on children of being 'saved' from factories and mines?

3 What was encouraged as a result of the Education Act (1870)?

4 Which Act abolished the practice of sending children under the age of fourteen to prison?

5 Which document first really recognised the rights of children?

6 What could the Plowden Report be credited with achieving?

7 What rights were stated in the UN Convention on the Rights of the Child (1989)?

8 Which statement in the Children Act (1989) acknowledges the rights of children?

9 Which standard from the National Standards relates directly to behaviour?

10 Give four arguments against smacking.

Part 2

Understanding behaviour – influences, consequences and positive management

Chapter 6

Influences on behaviour

Introduction

Before we can empower and guide children to manage their own behaviour, we need to understand some of the things that may influence behaviour. There are many influences on a child's behaviour, just as there are many influences on our own views and perceptions. Each of these influences affect each child differently as every child is unique. This chapter considers a range of influences that may change, shape or have an effect on a child and looks at theoretical perspectives underpinning some of these influences. The influences are divided into two categories:

◆ intrinsic influences

◆ external influences.

The chapter ends by considering an alternative way of looking at children's behaviour – the holistic approach.

Intrinsic influences

Intrinsic influences are those things that we are born with and are innate. Although much behaviour is learnt, as discussed in Chapter 2, there are some behaviours that appear to be innate, such as reflex behaviours in a newborn baby (e.g. startle) and those behaviours that may be the result of an inherited/genetic component (e.g. anything from how temperamental we are to how good we are at communicating). Conditions such as Tourette's syndrome, dyslexia and autistic disorder syndrome have all been found to have a genetic component.

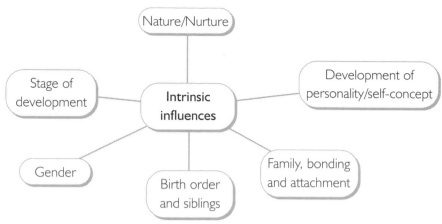

Intrinsic influences on behaviour

Nature/Nurture

As our scientific knowledge about human biology has increased, some scientists have begun to argue that many aspects of our development, such as our ability to learn, are genetically inherited. This has become known as the '**nature**' view. However, other scientists believe that humans are influenced more by their environment as they grow and develop. This has become known as the '**nurture**' view. The 'nature verses nurture' debate about development is still continuing.

The nature view

The nature view of development suggests that our skills are innate, inborn and instinctive. For example, the psychologist **Noam Chomsky** (born 1928) states that we are born with everything that we need to produce language and with the potential to understand the structure of any language. According to Chomsky, the process by which humans inherit language is known as a language acquisition device (L.A.D). On the other hand, another psychologist, Skinner, believed that children acquire language through operant conditioning; if the sounds that babies make are reinforced by another person, the child will learn to repeat them. Sounds that are not reinforced will be extinguished.

Humans inherit 23 pairs of chromosomes. There are probably between 60,000 and 80,000 genes altogether on these chromosomes. A person's genetic inheritance is a mixture of the genes from their parents and is called a **genotype**. A person who subscribes to the nature view would believe that most of a person's behaviour, intellect and personality is the result of their genotype and, as such, cannot be interfered with. If this argument is taken to its logical conclusion, it implies that humans have no 'free will' so need not be accountable for their actions. The nature view follows the idea that a child whose parent is a doctor, farmer, bricklayer or a footballer, for example, would inherit the skills necessary to follow that profession. In the same way, a parent can describe their child as having their grandfather's or grandmother's temper, or their father's eyes or mother's nose. Erikson believed that babies are born with some basic capabilities and distinct temperaments, but need to undergo dramatic changes before they can develop into adults.

The nurture view

Many psychologists believe that there are fundamental flaws in the nature view. While some accept that certain aspects of potential development, such as vision, are present from birth, they point out that humans do not always attain the prediction of their genotype; for example, children do not automatically follow the same profession as their parents, or have the same personality characteristics. Our experiences may have a far greater influence on our development than those characteristics that we inherit. The place where we live, the way we are brought up, the school we attend and the friendships we have can all influence how we learn and behave.

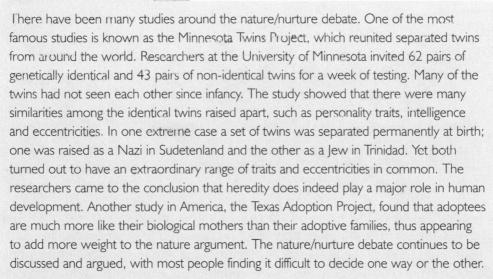

CASE STUDY

There have been many studies around the nature/nurture debate. One of the most famous studies is known as the Minnesota Twins Project, which reunited separated twins from around the world. Researchers at the University of Minnesota invited 62 pairs of genetically identical and 43 pairs of non-identical twins for a week of testing. Many of the twins had not seen each other since infancy. The study showed that there were many similarities among the identical twins raised apart, such as personality traits, intelligence and eccentricities. In one extreme case a set of twins was separated permanently at birth; one was raised as a Nazi in Sudetenland and the other as a Jew in Trinidad. Yet both turned out to have an extraordinary range of traits and eccentricities in common. The researchers came to the conclusion that heredity does indeed play a major role in human development. Another study in America, the Texas Adoption Project, found that adoptees are much more like their biological mothers than their adoptive families, thus appearing to add more weight to the nature argument. The nature/nurture debate continues to be discussed and argued, with most people finding it difficult to decide one way or the other.

What is your view?

1 Do you think, for example, that aggression is inherited, (a result of nature), or determined by influences in the environment (a result of nurture), or a combination of both?

2 Do 'intelligent' parents always have intelligent children?

3 Do you think that the sons of David Beckham, the former Manchester United and England footballer, will grow up to be a world-class footballers?

4 Will all the children who live on a run-down inner city estate, with high crime rates and juvenile delinquency, become criminals?

Development of personality/self-concept

Many people believe that a person's personality is inherited, and part of our genotype (the nature view). If we follow this line of thought it would mean that a person whose parents are outgoing and very sociable will be outgoing and very sociable. Similarly, shy parents will have shy children. However, does this mean that outgoing children inherit such traits or is it possible that they learn them from their parents? In the same way, does the child of shy parents inherit the shyness or is it behaviour learnt from their parents?

ACTIVITY

Read the following scenario and then try to answer the questions.

Jessie is five months old. Almost from birth she has been cross and irritable. She is restless and does not sleep for long periods, either at night or during the day. Often she is difficult to soothe. However, she can hold a toy, push herself up when laid on her front and is beginning to take puréed vegetables mixed with cereal from a spoon.

Jessie's mother, Mel, is very tired and suffering from lack of sleep. Her partner works long hours and other family members live some distance away. Before the baby was born Mel also worked long hours and had a stressful job. She often found it difficult to relax and 'switch off' from work when she came home, but she liked being busy and mentally active. She finds being at home with Jessie does not occupy her mind.

1 Which personality traits do you think Jessie may have inherited?
2 Can you think of two reasons why Jessie might be difficult to soothe?

Research has shown that a person's personality does not change that much as they mature. Humans do not mature very quickly compared to other species but all humans pass through the same stages of maturation and in the same order – but not at the same rate. As we mature we encounter new experiences which influence how we behave. For example, it is a normal part of growth and development for a baby or young child to be wary of strangers, but as children mature they usually become more confident and less wary of strangers. They also learn and develop strategies based on previous experiences to help them cope with new situations.

In Chapter 3 the views of Freud were considered in relation to how children learn and how their learning influences their personality and behaviour. Freud's theories are based on extensive case studies of his patients and this led him to the conclusion that much behaviour is the result of the unconscious mind. Delving into the unconscious mind requires skilled professional therapists and should not be attempted by untrained individuals.

Family, bonding and attachment

Many people believe that the family is one of the most powerful influences on children's behaviour. The vast majority of people in the Western world are born into a family, are reared by it and eventually form a new family of their own. Research in child development shows that the ways in which the family, especially parents, behave towards their children have a very great influence on almost every aspect of the child's development.

In the vast majority of families, parents love and care for their children, and if asked would probably say that they want the 'best' for their children. However, the style in which parents care for, love and meet their children's needs vary greatly from family to family and in different cultures. Some favour a more authoritarian style of parenting, where children are not expected to question their parents' views or reasons for doing things. Such parents often have high expectations of their children, but most children in this type of family benefit because there is a consistent approach.

Some parents and other family members may have expectations of a child that are not achievable – they are simply too high. This can lead to the child feeling worthless as they are continually failing to meet their parents' expectations; they may feel unloved and very inadequate about their own abilities. This will have a direct impact on their need to be loved, accepted and belong.

There are several psychological theoretical perspectives that attempt to explain attachments. They vary from those theories that claim attachment is instinctive (for example, a baby has an instinct, or innate need to bond with the person who cares and feeds it), to those theories that suggest that babies and young children bond and attach to individuals who help them develop and learn positive schemas (logical ideas and plans) about meeting their basic needs such as security and care. There is also the theory that children do not like being alone and so develop communication skills to keep other people near them, and so develop bonds and attachments.

It is usual for a baby of around eight months to have developed an attachment and bond with their primary caregiver. There are two recognised ways of assessing if the baby has developed a secure attachment:

1 If they are not afraid of the primary carer, but are afraid of strangers – stranger fear.
2 If they show distress or are upset when away from the person they are attached to – separation distress.

However, studies by **Rudi Schaffer** and **Peggy Emerson** in 1964 found that babies are able to make secure attachments with more than one person. This is usually referred to as having multiple attachments.

In the early years, attachment can be described as an emotional bond-link to the meeting of physiological needs, as identified by Maslow. By the time a child is three or four years old they are looking to bond with a person who provides stimulation as well as care and protection. During primary school years a child may form attachments with other children: peer groups often of the same sex who share their interests and friends. During teenage years the need for attachment may involve emotional security and social stimulation, and may include members of the opposite sex.

SNAPSHOT

Ellie is a private nanny. She takes the baby, aged eleven months, to the doctor, a new situation for the baby. When they sit down in the surgery the baby looks at Ellie's face to check her expression and response to the new situation. Ellie and the baby have a secure attachment and the baby can tell by Ellie's face if the situation is safe or something to be afraid of.

When attachments fail children may react in very different ways depending on the child's age/stage of development or personality. We must look at the whole child and use a holistic approach (see page 99). The following are some of the ways that some children may react to insecure or failed attachments:

◆ can be 'clingy'

◆ can display attention seeking behaviour

◆ can be aggressive and have angry 'scenes'

Birth order and siblings

The position of a child in a family – their birth order – is a factor that may affect their needs and development and therefore behaviour. A first-born child is in a revered but sometimes difficult position. There may be high parental expectations of this child, who has the undivided attention of their parents. Every milestone may be scrutinised and it is often the case that parents will have more photographs of their first-born as a baby and a toddler than of later children. It could be said that parents make all their mistakes on their first-born children, learning as they go along. Parents may be stricter and more anxious about their first-born, which may affect the child's need for independence and desire to belong to a peer group. First-borns may sometimes find that their superior position is threatened when a new sibling arrives. They may take it upon themselves to protect their younger siblings and in some ways 'police' their behaviour. It could be argued that by attempting to meet the safety needs of younger children, first-borns are satisfying their own need for esteem and recognition.

The youngest child, especially where there are three or more children in a family, does not have the responsibilities of his or her older siblings. Research shows that youngest children are often more successful than their brothers and sisters and may have a very individual approach and attitude to life. On the other hand, being the baby of a family can have its drawbacks. The youngest child may be slower to talk and may continue to show behaviours normally associated with younger children, such as lisping, thumb-sucking or using a comforter. One suggestion for this could be that since being the baby has certain privileges, such as more attention and more freedom, retaining 'baby-like' behaviours prolongs those privileges and satisfies the need for esteem.

Second or middle-born children may be born into a competitive atmosphere, trying to compete with the eldest child. Research has shown that many second-born children have characteristics and behaviours that are the exact opposite of the first-born. Thus the middle child may often be seen as the troublemaker, especially if the first-born is co-operative and obedient.

CASE STUDY

Michael, aged eight, was the middle of three children; his older brother was regarded as being academic, the younger sister was protected by her brothers and relied on them for her social activities. Michael's parents were asked to go into school to talk to the teacher as Michael had fallen behind with his school work and was often disruptive, displaying unacceptable behaviour. The teacher thought that Michael's problem was being the middle child: he couldn't compete academically with his brother and he felt responsible for his sister. The teacher felt that Michael needed to find something that he was good at and that he could do on his own without worrying about his sister. Michael had expressed an interest in swimming and so his parents decided that he could have swimming lessons. Over the next few months it became clear that Michael was going to be a very good swimmer; he joined the local swimming club and won several awards. His brother and sister did not join the club, although they occasionally did swim with him. Although Michael never achieved the same academic levels as his brother, he was successful in his own right. His behaviour at school gradually improved as he achieved greater success in swimming. This also coincided with his sister moving classes and Michael feeling less responsible for her.

1   How did Michael's birth order affect his development?

2   Apart from his birth order, can you think of any other reasons why Michael's behaviour could have become disruptive?

3   Why do you think Michael's behaviour improved along with his success in swimming?

4   Why was the fact that his sister moved classes significant for Michael?

Siblings

Siblings have an important part to play in the development of social relationships. Sibling rivalry, the competition between brothers and sisters, may be very powerful and in some cases may last into adult life. Almost every child has some feelings of jealousy, envy and rejection when they have to compete with a new baby who demands so much of the parents', or other family members' and carers', attention. The older child may feel unloved or rejected and this may lead to attention-seeking behaviour, much of which could be described as regressive, in order to gain the attention that was given automatically before the new baby's arrival. Children need to learn how to live together and develop independently, so it is important that each child has somewhere, a private place, regardless of size, where they can keep their things. In many ways a certain amount of competition and rivalry in older siblings is natural, but it should not become obsessive or destructive.

CASE STUDY

Grace did not see the need for her new baby brother. She thought that the family of Mum, Dad, herself, the dog and the hamster was big enough and asked, 'When is "it" going back?' Grace's grandparents started to take her out on her own to spend 'quality time' together, but these trips stopped when Grandad became ill. Grace became more and more jealous of the baby, doing everything that she could to try to prevent her parents giving him more attention. Grace is now nineteen years old, and her brother is fifteen. She still complains to her parents that, 'He gets far more than I did at his age. You didn't let me stay out that late when I was fifteen, you made me study. Can't he go to boarding school or something? He gets loads more money spent on him than I do.' Whilst her parents did not treat Grace and her brother exactly the same during their childhood, they do feel that each child was given a special part of their time and they did their best to meet each child's needs. Their view is that Grace has become obsessive in her perceived rivalry of her brother.

1 Why do you think Grace is jealous of her baby brother?

2 How would you deal with a child who is feeling jealous of their brother or sister?

3 What support could you offer them?

Gender

There has been much research into how a child develops gender identity. Although all children have their own individual needs, different societies and cultures have certain expectations of the sexes. Gender identity and roles are gradually acquired during childhood. Kohlberg suggested that gender identity is developed around thirty months, and is vital to future development, especially in response to the question, 'Who am I?' By the age of four years a child has usually divided their world into male and female and will show a preference for one role. By the age of seven a child is committed to shaping his or her behaviour to the cultural mould of what is 'appropriate' to his or her biological sex.

Children may become anxious and distressed if accused of acting in ways regarded as characteristic of the opposite gender, for example, if a boy is told he is behaving like a 'little girl' because he has cried. These messages can be so strong and pervasive in society that children spontaneously categorise themselves and the world in this way, for example, by preferring 'boys'' toys or 'girls'' colours. Cultures sometimes vary in their beliefs about gender roles, for example, some tribes in New Guinea promote the value of nurturing skills among boys, a characteristic considered feminine in Western society.

THINK IT OVER:

Will has just started a placement at a day nursery as part of his childcare and education course. He has already encountered comments such as, 'That's not a proper job for a man'. He feels that he has to prove to some of his female counterparts that he is as capable as them at caring for children and planning suitable activities. He is asked to plan a role-play area to help develop the nursery theme of 'People who help us'. He decides to make the area into a fire station, with telephones and message pads to encourage aspects of language development, dressing-up clothes and large boxes and blocks for the children to create a fire engine and so encourage imaginative play. He attempts to involve all of the children in planning and preparing the role-play area, but is aware that many girls are not as enthusiastic as some of the boys. His tutor suggests that Will talks to the children to try to find out why some of the girls are not so keen. Will discovers that some of the girls think that the role-play area will only be for the boys as 'You can only have firemen, not fire ladies.'

The nursery manager has already arranged for the children to visit the local fire station, so Will makes sure that their female fire officer will be on duty on the day of the children's visit. The visit proves to be very successful. The children are delighted at being allowed to clamber over the fire appliance and the female fire officer is able to show the girls and boys that she does the same job as the men, thereby helping them develop a greater understanding of non-stereotypical roles. When the children return to the nursery Will notices that both boys and girls are playing in the role-play area, with all of the children dressing up, 'driving' the fire engine and using the 'hoses'. Later, when the topic focus changes to 'the police', several children are heard to correct others, saying things like, 'it's not police *men* – it's police *officers*'. The nursery manager praises Will for how he has helped the children develop their ideas of gender roles, not least through being a positive role-model himself.

Stage of development

Individuals will have different needs at different stages of their development. A child's stage of development is a significant factor affecting their development, the satisfaction of their needs and ultimately their behaviour.

Under one year

Newborn babies are totally dependent on adults for all their needs. Very young babies have primitive reflexes, such as rooting, the Moro reflex and placing, which gradually disappear as they grow. In order for a young baby to grow and develop it is vital that their physiological needs are met. Babies who are undernourished or do not have their physiological needs satisfied will often, suffer from all-round developmental delay. They may not have the energy to play and actively

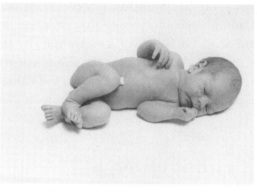

A newborn baby is totally dependent on his or her carers

explore. Babies need stimulation to explore their environment and, if this is not encouraged, they may be slow to develop mobility and cognitive skills. They also need to bond and form secure attachments with their main carers. If these attachments are not successfully developed the baby may have difficulties in satisfying their need to build relationships and belong to a group. Part of the bonding process usually involves the main carer communicating with the baby; this encourages language development and it could be argued that a child who has not formed secure bonds may have communication difficulties later in life. Physical contact when being changed, bathed and fed (all physiological needs) is an important part of the bonding process.

Young babies react to other people and situations with their entire bodies. They gradually become conscious of themselves as separate from others. With this awareness young babies also learn that they have influence upon and are influenced by others. For example a baby will very quickly learn that if they make enough noise, someone, usually their main carer, will come and give them attention and meet their needs.

One to two years

A mobile, active baby or toddler needs to have their safety needs met, but must still have their basic needs satisfied in order to continue to develop in a healthy way. Children of this age often do not often have a sense of danger and so require good supervision. Piaget describes children of this age as egocentric. Egocentric children see themselves as being at the centre of their environment and as such have no understanding of the consequences of their actions. They do, however, watch and observe other children and adults and will imitate those around them. (Look back at Bandura's theory in Chapter 2, page 17).

Young children between eighteen months and two years show increasing independence and make every effort to get responses from adults and other children. This can be clearly seen in the responses of young children when they receive praise.

Toddlers are egocentric by nature

Two to three years

The behaviour of children in this age group is often characterised by 'temper tantrums', frustrated outbursts and bouts of impatience. Children of this age have a need to become more independent not just socially but in other areas of development such as the control of the bladder and bowels. However, this need for independence is limited by their physical and cognitive skills – hence the frustration. Children of this age need consistency from the adults around them in order for them to be able to understand behaviour boundaries. As with all children, their physiological needs dominate at certain times; however, children of this age can begin to understand that they may have to wait for a meal, for example, and can't have everything that they want immediately.

The 'terrible twos' are frustrating for children and adults

Children of this age need to understand what they can do independently, such as pour their own drinks; to have this understanding it is important that children have relationships that help them develop self-confidence, positive self-esteem and a belief in themselves and their abilities. Adults who have clear and consistent expectations and who trust in a child's abilities can help them do this.

SNAPSHOT

Will planned to turn the role-play area into a fire station. During circle time he talked to the children about what resources and equipment they would need to have in the play area. He encouraged all of the children in the group to take part and make a contribution and praised them to show that he valued their views and opinions.

Three to four years

Most children of this age have begun some form of social interaction with their peers, at such places as pre-school groups and nurseries. At times the need to belong to a social or peer group may be dominant; but if the child has not established secure attachment and bonds earlier in their life they may find this difficult. Many early years establishments have key worker systems, which allow children to form bonds with one person. Some children who have established secure bonds

Social interaction with other children becomes important at this age

with one main carer, for example, their mother, may suffer from separation anxiety when separated. The child may feel frightened and unsafe; their safety need may not be satisfied and this could lead to unacceptable behaviour or even a failure to thrive. An effective key worker system should enable a young child to develop a strong relationship with another caring adult, so the child will develop a sense of stability when separated from their main carer.

Four to five years

Most children of this age play with their peers quite happily and are now able to communicate their views and feelings. They start to be concerned about how others see them and respond well to praise and encouragement. As children's language and cognitive skills develop and as they become less self-orientated they can play games with rules which require them to consider the views and needs of others. Their social skills are usually well developed and they can use language to express themselves. However, children of this age are also often starting full-time education and this experience can be a significant influence on their behaviour. Some children take to school routine without any difficulties or problems; but others appear to regress in their development. The fear for their own safety and preservation during periods of separation may become dominant. For example, a child who does not know where the toilets are or how they are going to get their lunch (the satisfaction of basic needs) may become very fearful, anxious and distressed.

Five years plus

Bandura's social learning theory can be very evident in this age group as children copy both the appropriate *and* inappropriate aspects of the behaviour of their peers. At the same time, if Kohlberg's theory is correct, children also understand the difference between right and wrong, the threat of some form of punishment being a good reason for behaving in an acceptable way. Children may be between Stage 3 and Stage 4 of Kohlberg's sequence of moral development. (See page 35 in Chapter 3.)

School-age children learn to talk about their emotions and feelings, and this is an important part of their mental health; however, it can be very challenging for some children if they have not resolved the crises of earlier stages. It is important that children develop a positive self-image and a sense of competence so that they can approach puberty and adolescence with confidence.

Starting school is a big step for young children

Peer pressure can be a significant factor in the development of school-age children

External influences

External influences on behaviour are those significant events or changes that occur in our lives or are part of our environment. Sometimes we have some control over these events, such as a planned hospital stay or starting at a new school, but often these events or changes happen without warning, such as a bereavement. Change in any shape or form, planned or unplanned, influences behaviour, but it is always important to remember that all children are different and react to changes in different ways.

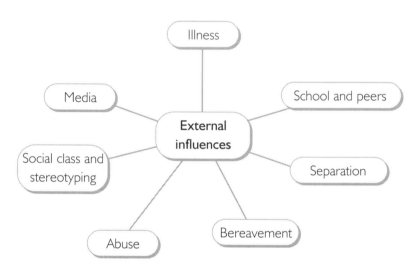

External influences on behaviour

Illness (including hospitalisation)

One of the aims of every parent and adult working with children should be to keep children as healthy as possible at all times. We actively work to make sure that the environment that children are in is hygienic and as infection-free as possible. However, all children at some time in their lives suffer from some form of illness. Any illness is stressful for a child and their family, but the severity of its effect depends on the illness itself and its treatment, how the family copes with the illness and whether the illness necessitates a period of hospitalisation. Short-term and acute illnesses that do not last very long do not usually significantly affect a child's overall development, whereas a chronic illness or long-term condition, which restricts a child in some way, may affect their overall development and behaviour. For example, the child may seek attention, perhaps as a way of overcoming fears or seeking reassurance, and they may lack confidence, become withdrawn and regress in their social skills and development.

Read the following scenario and then answer the questions.

Karen is a private nanny working for a family with three children, a girl aged five years, a boy of two and a half and a baby. The baby was born prematurely and has spent a lot of time in hospital. This has been a very anxious time for both parents who have relied a lot on Karen to care for the other two children. The little boy had been toilet trained before the birth of the baby, but since her arrival has had many 'accidents'. The teacher of the older child has told Karen that she has become quite aggressive towards other children, often hitting out, especially when she can't have her own way.

1 Why do you think the little boy is having 'accidents'?

2 Why do you think the older child is behaving in this way?

3 What can Karen and the parents do to help the older children?

4 How can Karen help the younger child regain bowel and bladder control?

Hospitalisation

The effects of hospitalisation for any length of time on children and their families should not be underestimated, especially an emergency one. In the past, hospitals had strict visiting times for parents, other children were not allowed into the wards and medical procedures were not fully explained to either parents or the child. Following the work of **John Bowlby** on the effects of attachment, **James** and **Joyce Robertson** produced several very distressing films in the 1950s, showing the effects of separation on children in hospitals and residential day care settings. The films graphically showed the emotional distress, and in some cases deprivation, suffered by the children. As a

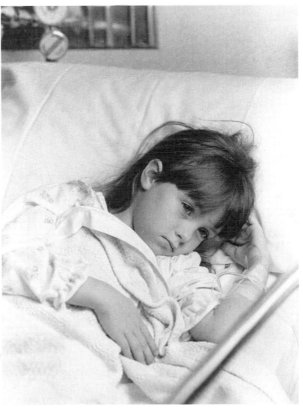

Hospitals can seem frightening places to a sick child

result the medical profession began to slowly change its procedures and today parents are involved as much as possible. Many hospitals now employ play therapists to work alongside medical staff and have named nurses to work with specific children. However, this good practice does not mean that children are not adversely affected by hospital stays. For many people, hospitals are unknown places, the procedures are unfamiliar and there are many new people to meet, in addition to feelings of fear about operations or illness. All of this threatens an individual's need for security and personal safety.

School and peers (including bullying)

Starting school, nursery or a pre-school group can be a major event in a child's life. For most children it is the first time that they come into contact with such large numbers of other children, of different ages, backgrounds and cultures. The social influences of school life are considered to be very powerful. Evidence of the social learning theory discussed in Chapter 2 can be clearly seen in many classrooms and playgrounds in our schools.

All schools have a behaviour policy in some form that sets out how children are expected to behave. The way in which the policy is implemented influences how the children behave just as much as the actual content of the policy, such as no running in corridors. Most children of statutory school age spend approximately 30 hours each week in school. Most of that time teachers and other school staff dictate how children spend their time – in academic lessons, for instance, or play and sporting activities – but all children are expected to show some level of independence and responsibility and conform to the behaviour policy. Teachers reinforce some behaviours and 'punish' others, thus making them seem powerful to young children. Again the social learning is evident as children see their teachers as positive role models.

Four-year-olds may not be mature enough to cope with the demands of full-time school in infant classes. The school may be a much larger place than they have experienced before with fewer adults to support them. This inability to cope will affect and influence their behaviour.

Peer group

A peer group is a group of friends of a similar age who spend time together and participate in co-operative activities. Peer groups may be a very powerful influence on behaviour and social development. Many people can probably relate to situations where they behave very differently with their peers from the way they do with family members or people that they meet at work. For example, a teenager may be uncommunicative and unresponsive towards his or her parents, but when with their peers may be animated, lively and very talkative.

Studies have shown that babies as young as three months old respond to other babies of a similar age. Babies at around six months squeal, smile and reach out to touch their peers. As children mature, the exchanges between their peers become longer and more co-ordinated, for example, three-year-olds begin to share and co-operate when playing. They may copy each other's actions and behaviour. By the time children are about five years old they choose to participate in group activities with their peers and are beginning to be influenced more powerfully by the needs and expectations of the peer group.

One of the most widely-held beliefs is that peer groups control the behaviour of children, sometimes more than parents and teachers – particularly the case with teenagers. On occasions peer group relationships and expectations do cause children stress. All children want to 'belong', and the fear of not 'belonging' or being accepted by peers may influence a child's behaviour. Wearing the 'right' type of clothes or listening to a specific type of music may become a vital part of belonging. Sometimes this need to belong and conform to the peer group is in conflict with what parents or schools expect from children.

Peers are prime candidates for prompting imitation in children; for example, if a child sees one of their peers playing aggressively with toys, the child also plays aggressively. As well as providing models for some behaviour, peers may actively reinforce certain behaviours. Peer groups often have clear 'rules' about which social behaviours are acceptable and those which are not. Children behave in a way that enables them to be a part of their peer group, so that behaviour is reinforced by the acceptance of their peers. Peer groups can be influential in, and used for, transmitting cultural values; groups such as Rainbows, Brownies, Cubs and Scouts are based on peer groups and encourage children to behave in ways that reflect certain values. Some societies foster and encourage peer group identity among children in the form of activity camps or groups, such as 'Pioneer camps' in Russia and kibbutzim in Israel.

CASE STUDY

A group of girls at school are devoted fans of one particular boy band and avidly collect posters, cards, CDs and newspaper reports about their 'heroes'. Jalah is also very keen on the same boy band and wants to be part of the group of fans. However, Jalah's parents have forbidden her to mix with this group of girls as they consider them to be a 'bad influence 'on their daughter. Unknown to her parents Jalah does spend time with these girls. Jalah's mother finds a poster of the band in her daughter's bag and accuses Jalah of disobeying her parents. Jalah tells her mother that the other girls have put the poster there because they don't like her and want to get her into trouble.

1 Why did Jalah lie?

2 How can she reconcile the wishes of her parents and her desire to be like her peers?

Bullying

Bullies may be frustrated children who have experienced bullying themselves in other situations. Bullying others may often be a cry for help, an attempt at attention-seeking, or a way of exercising control over others. Bullies often select their victims because they know that bullying others will increase their feelings of control and power. Children who are the victims of bullies need to have their self-esteem and confidence increased and their need for safety and security met.

Bullying is a type of abuse which can take many forms such as:

- name-calling and verbal abuse
- fighting or physical attacks
- not allowing a child to participate in activities with the peer group
- racial and discriminatory remarks
- threats.

There are many other forms of bullying, all of which can result in distress and emotional problems for the child concerned. Often this stress manifests itself in changes in the ways a child normally behaves. In some cases a child may become withdrawn, uncommunicative and antisocial. Tragically, some bullied children become so desperate that they take their own lives. Many children show developmental regression, such as bed-wetting, thumb-sucking, and have communication and language difficulties. Some children suffer disturbed sleep and nightmares. Bullying is a very serious issue and children who are being bullied – and those who are bullies – need help, understanding and care in order to manage their behaviour effectively.

Bullying varies in severity and in the response that it provokes. For this reason, it can sometimes be difficult to differentiate between children who are boisterous, rough and thoughtless and those who want to go about bullying. Many schools have developed a separate policy on bullying as distinct from their behaviour policy. Such policies should involve all members of the school from governors to children, and clearly set out procedures that can be followed when bullying occurs. As with all policies and procedures, ways of dealing with bullies and those being bullied must be applied consistently.

Separation (including divorce and imprisonment of a parent/carer)

The effects of separation and the distinct stages through which a child may move were discussed in Chapter 3. However, the behavioural effects of a divorce or imprisonment of a parent have a specific significance.

Divorce

Many children experience separation from one parent as a result of divorce. Although it is possible for parents to have joint custody and care and control of the children, it is often the case that the father leaves the family home. The behavioural effects of divorce on children depend on many factors such as:

1 The age of the child – research by **Wallerstein** and **Kelly** in 1980 showed that pre-school children display the most severe and immediate effects. However, the long-term effects of divorce are more pronounced in older children.

2 Their gender – boys show more distress than girls, especially if separated from their father before the age of five.

3 The amount of disruption to their lives, such as having to adjust to two households.

4 The quality of the relationships and attachments with the parents before the divorce.

As it was similarly cautioned before, children will not necessarily show negative behaviour when parents divorce; some may, some may not, and many cope with the change in their circumstances with minimal effects on their behaviour.

Imprisonment

In many ways the behavioural effects of having a parent in prison are the same as in the case of divorce, in that the child is separated from one of their parents. However, in the case of divorce a child usually maintains contact with that parent. Although children and partners can visit the parent in prison, the time together is restricted. In some cases the results of imprisonment may mean that other family members or foster carers care for a child. This can be considered almost a form of bereavement for the child, who may lose contact with their parent for some length of time. Some children, especially older children, may feel very angry that their parent has left them; younger children may not fully understand the circumstances and may become distressed, fretful and anxious.

Bereavement

Feelings of loss and grief were once not generally recognised in young children except in extreme cases, and it was common practice to exclude young children from the death and grieving process. We now recognise that children need to grieve in their own individual way. The death of a parent, sibling or close family member may be a significant and profound loss. But, equally, for many children, starting school, a change in the environment such as moving house, a primary carer returning to work, or separation from a parent (through divorce, separation, imprisonment or hospitalisation) can all cause stress and for many children a sense of loss. Children may grieve for their key worker after they have moved from nursery to school, or for their friend who lived next door before they moved house. Some people view these forms of loss as relatively trivial, minor losses, so sometimes children are not given the help and support that they may need. Minor losses cannot be easily defined: to some children, losing their favourite soft toy in a shopping complex is a significant loss, likewise the death of a pet. Reaction to death and loss very much depends on the age of the child and their level of understanding.

Babies may show signs of separation anxiety when they 'pick up' on the emotional feelings of adults around them and become unsettled and fretful. Young children often do not understand the physical finality of death and may ask when the person who has died is coming back. Some children may feel responsible for the person 'going away'; some may act out the situation in play or search for the person who has died. Older children may also think that they are responsible for the death or loss and may feel guilty. Some children feel angry that the person has left them. Often these emotions show themselves in changes in a child's behaviour, such as aggressive or angry outbursts or withdrawal.

Children who have experienced loss need sensitive adults who will spend time allowing them to talk about their feelings, to play and act out situations about emotions, and who will answer all questions with honesty. There are several distinct stages of loss and grief that we all move through, although there are no clear-cut descriptions of how we will react or behave as we pass through these stages. Some adults and children when dealing with the death of a close family member want to talk about the person, others do not want to talk; some may cry openly, others may not cry at all. We are all individual and we react and behave in individual ways.

ACTIVITY

Look at the stages of grief (in the flow-chart opposite) and the examples given of the reactions of someone who has lost their purse or wallet. Try to work out what you think might be the reactions of:

◆ a three-year-old child who has lost their favourite toy

◆ a six-year-old whose grandfather has just died.

The flow-chart below is a way of summarising how a person behaves when they have lost someone or something.

The stages of grief	Example
Shock	*I feel physically sick, cold, clammy, sweaty*
↓	
Disbelief	*I can't possibly have lost my wallet/purse*
↓	
Denial	*I must have left it somewhere*
↓	
Anger	*I am so stupid, why didn't you remind me to pick it up?*
↓	
Guilt	*I feel guilty that I have caused so much hassle/trouble*
↓	
Self-recrimination	*I blame myself, I should be more careful*
↓	
Depression	*I won't be able to sort everything out*
↓	
Idealisation	*That was the best wallet/purse I ever had*
↓	
Acceptance	*I will just have to get on with things*

Abuse

Abuse may have long-term effects. Children who are subjected to repeated abuse may suffer severe psychological damage and be seriously damaged for the rest of their lives. Many adults who suffered abuse may have problems parenting their own children. Some children are more vulnerable to abuse than others, for example:

◆ a child who has previously been abused
◆ a child who cries a lot
◆ a child who is difficult to feed
◆ a child who has not formed secure attachments with its mother
◆ a child who is the oldest sibling in the family
◆ a child with a disability.

This does not mean to say that every child who fits one or more of the above criteria will be abused.

There are four main forms of abuse:

◆ physical
◆ sexual

◆ neglect

◆ emotional/psychological.

There are definite behaviour signs and symptoms of each form of abuse. Some of these are summarised in the table below.

Physical NB: There is a very fine line between reasonable chastisement such as smacking and physical abuse; many people believe that any form of physical chastisement is a form of physical abuse.	• Becoming withdrawn and uncommunicative • Engaging in aggressive play, often towards other children and in role play • Using aggressive responses towards adults • Being unable to sit comfortably, or sitting with unusual stiffness • Showing reluctance to join in physical play
Sexual	• Using sexual language and knowledge of sexual behaviour not normally associated with a child of that age • Showing insecurity • Clinging to trusted adults and at the same time showing an unwillingness to be in the company of particular adults • Immature actions for their age, such as comfort habits like rocking, thumb-sucking and wanting a comforter • Using imaginary play to act out sexual behaviour • Undressing themselves at inappropriate times or exposing the genital area • Drawing or painting images of a sexual nature • Becoming withdrawn and uncommunicative
Neglect NB: This means failing to provide adequate food, shelter or clothing, in other words a failure to meet a child's basic physical and psychological needs. The child is literally abandoned to look after themselves.	• Talking about looking after younger siblings and taking on responsibilities at home not normally expected of children of their age – i.e. being stressed by a sense of responsibility • Talking about being left alone – i.e. showing fear and insecurity
Emotional/psychological	• Lacking self-esteem, showing low self-confidence • Becoming withdrawn and uncommunicative • Attention-seeking, such as deliberately being unco-operative, troublesome, telling lies or clinging to an adult and craving attention • Responding easily to any sort of attention – even if that attention is another form of abuse • Showing behaviour usually associated with a younger child, such as having 'temper tantrums' at an age when normally they would not behave in this way

It is a fact that children who are physically or psychologically abused within their family are more likely to have insecure attachments than non-abused children. Abusive parents or other family members tend to react negatively to their child's attempts to build relationships, by not responding to smiles or facial expressions, for instance. Abused children develop a fear of the abuser, an emotion that does not allow stable secure attachments to be formed. It may be very difficult for a child to tell another person outside the family about the abuse, or even recognise that the abuse is not 'normal' family practice.

It has been proved that abuse within a family is frequently the result of past experiences of the abusers; an abused child may become an abuser, not only of their own children, but sometimes of younger siblings. Everyone working with children has a duty of care to keep children safe from abuse and should therefore know the procedures to follow if abuse is suspected.

Social class and stereotyping

In the twenty-first century it can be argued that that we are, or should be, living in a classless society; but, in reality, this is not strictly true. There are still those who believe, for example, that if they pay for private education or private healthcare they will be getting a better service, and, similarly, that those who can afford to pay for these services are better paid, have more disposable income and are therefore in a higher 'class' than others. In some communities there is still a belief that speaking in a certain way, using a particular dialect or accent, places a person in a different class from another. What effect can this have on a child's development?

THINK IT OVER:

What are your own views about class?

Do you think that the development of a child or children of a single parent living on benefits will be adversely affected compared to the child or children of parents living in a detached house in a suburb? Would you assume that the single parent would be of a lower social class than the other parents?

Sometimes the views and beliefs of a person are not formed as a result of their past experiences, but as a result of stereotyping. Stereotyping could be defined as a way of labelling, or having a fixed image of something or someone; for example, saying that all people who enjoy watching and studying birds are boring and wear woolly bobble hats. Stereotyping may make us believe that individuals will always behave in a certain way. For example, if we think that all fat people are lazy, then we will think that a fat child is a lazy child. However, often these views are formed before we really get to know the person in question, and once we have more knowledge we may understand that our views are not correct. Making judgements based on stereotypes is a form of prejudice, which leads to discrimination. It is important that all people working with children provide activities and experiences that help children develop opinions and views that are not based on stereotypes. For example, we should make it clear that Red Indians (who are in fact various tribes of North American Indians) do not all live in tepees; just as Eskimos (who prefer to be called Inuits) do not all live in igloos.

SNAPSHOT

Geraint had behavioural difficulties in primary school and his teacher found, at times, it was difficult to help him to manage his behaviour. Geraint's older sister had also experienced difficulties at the school. When Geraint's younger brother started school, the teacher admitted that she had a stereotypical view of the family – having children with behavioural difficulties – when in fact this was not true once she got to know the younger boy. However, the teacher admitted that at first she was 'hard' on the boy because she expected problems. This led to him displaying a certain reluctance to join in some activities, because he thought he was going to 'get into trouble'.

ACTIVITY

In your view, is social class a factor affecting a child's behaviour and development?

Read the following short scenarios and then see if you can answer the question above.

1 Jan and James are both professionals, working full-time in the city, and they employ a qualified childcare worker to care for their children.

2 Hari is divorced and cares for his son himself. He gave up his job as a retail manager after his divorce.

3 Tom has ADHD. He has two older brothers. His mother works part-time in a supermarket and his father fits double-glazed windows. Money is very tight.

4 Melodie achieved 9 'A' grades in her GCSEs. Her father, a GP, and mother, a social worker, were delighted. Then Melodie announced that she was pregnant and wanted to keep her baby. She would then be a single mum living on benefits.

5 Sunil and Ameera moved from Camden Town in London with their parents to Belfast in Northern Ireland. The whole family pronounce words differently to the people around them in Belfast, partly due to their 'London accents and dialect'.

Media

Concern about the influence of popular media on children has a long history. More than 5,000 years ago, the ancient philosopher Plato proposed to ban poets from his ideal republic, because he feared that their stories about immoral behaviour would corrupt young minds. In modern times, pressure groups have tried to 'protect' children from popular literature, the music hall, the cinema, comics, television and video 'nasties'. According to most studies, the vast majority of children watch several hours of television and/or videos each day. Recent research in America suggests that by the age of 14 the 'average' American child has seen 11,000 murders on television. Any child switching on a television has an extraordinarily high chance of seeing some form of violent behaviour. Studies have shown that during prime-time television, there are five to six acts of physical aggression per hour and this number is even higher at weekends. Bandura's experiment with the Bobo doll (see page 17) reinforced the view that children are influenced by the media and there was much debate in the 1990s regarding the influence of videos on young children following the violent murder of the toddler Jamie Bulger by two ten-year-olds. Televisions, DVDs and computers are now common items in a child's bedroom. It is not surprising that the influence of the media is considerably more powerful today than it was 20 years ago.

Some researchers suggest that frequent viewing of violent television over a period of time conditions the viewer gradually to accept violence as normal, dulling their sensitivity to aggressive behaviour in everyday life. This is usually referred to as **desensitisation**. Television viewing may influence not only behaviour but also the development of attitudes and values; for example, a strong and powerful character in a programme may behave in a threatening way to a younger, weaker character and so give the message to some children that it is acceptable to 'bully' younger and weaker children.

However, it must be remembered that children are influenced in both positive and negative ways and some aspects of the media may influence children to behave in socially acceptable ways. Television programmes promote many early literacy and numeracy skills, and they help children understand social issues and promote socially acceptable values. Many media personalities positively influence the behaviour of children, for example, by becoming involved in charity appeals to help others.

Holistic development

We have seen how a child's behaviour may be influenced by intrinsic and external factors. However, it can be argued that the most accurate way of understanding a child's behaviour is to understand how children grow and develop in all areas, or holistically. This is a relatively new form of scientific study.

Some adherents categorise development into five main areas:

1 physical
2 intellectual
3 language
4 emotional
5 social.

Some people put language and intellectual together, some combine emotional and social, some add another category of cultural developments see, for example, the four 'aspects' listed in the 'Birth to Three Matters' Framework (page 67).

It does not really matter how we decide to categorise development; what is important is to remember that all aspects, areas or components of a child's development are inter-related and as such are interdependent on each other. This is especially important when considering behaviour. In other words, a child's behaviour depends on the inter-relation at any one time between a number of simultaneous aspects of development – with each one perhaps affected by a different influence.

For example, a lack of communication (language) on the part of a child may cause concern, and could manifest itself in angry outbursts and acts of frustration. However, the reason for the lack of communication might be due to the child's lack of self-confidence. In such a situation we might attempt to increase the child's language skills by focusing on developing the child's self-confidence through achievable goals and lots of praise. We must consider the whole child when looking at behaviour, as there is the danger that we will focus on only one aspect of development when the antecedents of the behaviour might be a combination of several aspects.

SNAPSHOT

Tom, aged five, was becoming disruptive in the classroom and rarely finished set tasks. The teacher and classroom assistant decided to focus on developing his concentration skills. They had little success and so arranged to meet with Tom's mother. It became clear that Tom had become disruptive at home, and a chance remark by his mother, 'He never listens to me', prompted the teacher to consider whether Tom could actually hear. Subsequent tests showed that Tom in fact couldn't hear clearly (possibly as a result of a bad cold and chest infection earlier in the year). It was an aspect of Tom's physical development that had been affecting the way he behaved, and not just a lack of concentration. He had become frustrated and disruptive because he couldn't hear, and he hadn't finished tasks because he hadn't heard what he was expected to do.

CHECKPOINT

1 What is the difference between nature and nurture?

2 How can high parental expectations of a child affect their behaviour?

3 How could being the second or middle-born child in a family affect behaviour?

4 When does Kohlberg suggest children develop gender identity?

5 How might the siblings of a sick child be affected by the illness?

6 Give one example of how the work of James and Joyce Robertson has affected medical procedures.

7 How could the need to belong to a peer group cause conflict?

8 List five forms of bullying.

9 What are the four main forms of abuse?

10 What is desensitisation?

Chapter 7

Promoting positive behaviour

Introduction

Most children want to behave in appropriate and acceptable ways and to please the adults around them. In reality, it is only a minority of children that display behaviour that causes concern. Whilst it is very important that adults working with children understand how to manage unwanted behaviours and guide children, it is also essential that every opportunity be taken to promote positive behaviour. The ways in which a child behaves can be changed or modified through encouraging positive behaviour using some of the theories discussed in Part 1, perhaps, for example, with some form of reward, and discouraging unwanted or negative behaviours. It must be remembered that at all times we should be encouraging and guiding a child to manage their own behaviour. If one strategy does not appear to be effective then we must be prepared to try something else to promote positive behaviour.

This chapter will consider:

◆ relating theory to practice

◆ effective strategies to promote positive behaviour including empowerment

◆ non-effective strategies

◆ the use of drugs to manage children's behaviour.

Relating theory to practice

Positive behaviour can be promoted in a variety of ways:

◆ The **social learning** theory discussed in Part 1 emphasised the importance of good, positive role models. Adults have a vital role to play in creating an atmosphere and environment where inappropriate and negative behaviour is exceptional. We should always try to be positive role models for all children. Adults cannot expect children to talk to each other in calm voices, if they shout at children. Similarly, adults who hit, use inappropriate language, or hurt other people should not expect children to behave any differently.

SNAPSHOT

Toby, aged eight, and his little brother, eighteen months, were being cared for by their grandmother during the school holidays. Toby was bored; in his view his brother was getting all Gran's attention, so during a shopping trip he started messing about in the store. Gran told him to stop it, but he ignored her. She told Toby again to 'behave' and again he ignored her. This went on for several minutes. Finally Gran lost her patience and shouted angrily at Toby. The little brother immediately copied the angry sound of Gran's voice. For the rest of the day, each time the toddler wanted to get Toby's attention or Gran's, he shouted, using the same tone of voice as Gran had used. He had learnt that to get attention he needed to shout angrily. This is an example of the social learning theory in action.

◆ The **behaviourist** theories state that children learn by being rewarded. Childcare workers can promote positive behaviour by rewarding children for demonstrating acceptable and appropriate behaviour. The rewards can be varied; some settings use verbal praise, some use star charts, and some use a combination of both. Another effective way to promote positive behaviour is simply to ignore inappropriate behaviour. Of course, sometimes this can be difficult and if the behaviour places another individual at risk, then it cannot be ignored.

SNAPSHOT

The classroom assistant and teacher of a Year 3 class wanted to reward children for positive behaviours. Both adults found it difficult to ignore unacceptable behaviours. They decided that every time a child behaved in an acceptable way, a marble would be placed in a jar; when the jar was full, all of the class would be rewarded with a treat such as extra-long story time, longer playtime, free choice of activity for part of the afternoon, or sometimes special biscuits or something similar. Marbles were taken out of the jar if a child did not behaviour appropriately or in an acceptable way. In that case the treat would take longer to materialise.

The 'marble in the jar' idea uses behaviourist theory, with children learning by being rewarded, and also social learning theory and peer group pressure. If a child did something that caused a marble to be removed, they came under pressure from their peers and could also see that the reward and ultimate treat materialised if they copied the actions of the children who did behave in acceptable and appropriate ways.

◆ Maslow's theory (see page 39) shows us that certain needs must be met if we are to develop into emotionally and socially mature individuals. Children need **security**. This can be interpreted in a number of ways: children need to be protected from harm; they need to feel safe; and they benefit from the security of a routine, for example, knowing what will happen next. This can be applied to behaviour by setting boundaries or having rules about what is acceptable and what is not. A child needs to fully understand the boundaries or rules so that they can also understand what will happen if they go 'past' the boundary or break a rule. Therefore the explanation of rules and boundaries must be in language that is appropriate to the child's age and stage of development. Children need to be involved in setting boundaries, so that they can understand why the boundaries and/or rules exist. Any rule or boundary that is set for a child must be applied consistently.
Any inconsistency will lead to feelings of insecurity.

SNAPSHOT

A nursery class has 24 children at each of its morning and afternoon sessions. The staff have developed a routine for each session which is reproduced below.

	Morning		Afternoon
9:00	Registration Circle time	12:45	Registration Circle time
9:20	Free choice of pre-planned activities	1:05	Free choice of pre-planned activities
10:25	Tidy-up time	2:10	Tidy-up time
10:30	Circle time – sharing of experiences	2:15	Circle time – sharing of experiences
10:45	Outdoor play or vigorous indoor play if weather is bad	2:30	Outdoor play or vigorous indoor play if weather is bad – free play
11:10	Story time and songs and rhymes	2:55	Story time and songs and rhymes
11:30	Children go home	3:15	Children go home

Children have free access to snacks, drinks and toilets throughout both sessions to meet their individual needs.

The staff try as much as possible to stick to this routine and make a conscious effort to tell the children five minutes before the end of an activity that it is about to end and to say what will happen next. They have found that new children quickly begin to anticipate what the next activity will be and the staff believe that this helps the children to feel secure and therefore settled in the nursery environment. The routine has been printed out on to two pieces of large card, one for the morning and one for the afternoon, and is displayed on the wall near the reading area. There are clock faces showing the times of changes next to each activity, with a picture to show what the children will be doing. The staff use this display to help the children learn the routine and anticipate the next activity.

ACTIVITY

Now compare the routine in your work setting with the example in the snapshot above. Make a note of the similarities and differences.

1 In what ways do you think your workplace routine helps children to feel secure?

2 Do you tell the children what is going to happen next?

3 If not, is there a good reason for this?

4 If your work setting does not have a routine, can you think of other ways that your workplace helps children to develop a sense of security?

5 Put together a routine that would be effective in your setting.

The child psychologist **Dr Richard Woolfson** uses the phrase 'pro-social-behaviour' to describe behaviours that are positive and altruistic, or selfless. He suggests that there are three main features to altruistic behaviour:

◆ Sharing – when a person shares out part of their personal belongings or possessions, even though there is no obvious personal benefit

◆ Co-operation – when the behaviour of a person is instrumental in gaining a reward that is shared by others (such as the marble in the jar)

◆ Empathy – when a person experiences the emotional state of another person and understands their feelings and emotions.

Dr Woolfson suggests that children can be encouraged to behave in a pro-social way as part of everyday activities in whatever setting, and by learning from positive role models (social learning theory). Pro-social behaviour can also be encouraged through formal 'training packages' to help children learn anti-bullying strategies.

Try out these activities in your work setting, and see how they encourage pro-social/altruistic behaviour.

1 Put a piece of newspaper on the floor and tell the children that they all have to place at least one foot and one hand on the paper. The smaller the piece of paper and the larger the group the more challenging the game. This game encourages co-operation, sharing and lots of fun!

2 Get a large clean empty plastic bottle. Get six large pencils; make sure that the diameter of each pencil is slightly less than the opening of the bottle. Firmly tie one end of a piece of string around the top of the pencil and lower it into the bottle leaving the other end of the string hanging out of the bottle; repeat for all of the pencils. Six children hold onto the loose end of each piece of string. The aim of the game is to get all of the pencils out of the bottle in the shortest possible time. To do this the children must co-operate with each other totally.

Effective strategies to promote positive behaviour (including empowerment)

We will now look at some strategies for working with children that have proved to be effective in helping them manage their behaviour. These strategies are probably the most commonly used and have proved to be effective with many children most of the time. However, it must always be remembered that because one strategy works effectively for one child, the same strategy may not be effective with another child. All children are different and unique, and we should strive to meet the individual needs of all children in our care. We must be flexible and be prepared to try a variety of strategies in order to help children. However, it is not good practice to use more than one strategy at any one time. This leads to inconsistencies and confuses a child.

Deciding on a strategy

Before any strategy is implemented, it is good practice to decide which behaviour is causing most concern or stress. Practical ways of doing this are discussed in Chapter 8 in more detail. It is not practical to attempt to change all the inappropriate behaviours by using one or more strategies all at once; it is best to select just one behaviour and one consistent strategy to work on at first.

For example, a child may be causing concern in the classroom because they are inattentive and disruptive, they shout out and they constantly demand attention. In such a situation we could decide that we want to deal with the shouting out by not appearing to react, while rewarding the child with verbal praise when they put up their hand to offer an answer or want to say something.

When progress has been made, in other words the incidences of shouting out have decreased, we may move towards implementing another strategy to help the child manage another aspect of their behaviour. Using the example above, we might decide to help the child develop concentration skills, and so help them to be more attentive. The strategy we could use could be based on the social learning theory, such as including the child in small group games with children with good concentration skills, and again rewarding the child when they concentrate.

Remember, using more than one strategy to try to change more than one behaviour is very confusing for both the adult and the child – not to mention being hard work.

Before any strategy is considered there are three important steps that you should follow:

Step 1
Find out if anything is bothering or worrying the child. In other words, try to find out the antecedents and possible influences or reasons for this behaviour?

You may have to use a range of methods to find out about a child's worries and concerns, for example, talking, drama or role-play. Younger children may not be able to express themselves verbally to fully explain how they feel. In such situations it may be helpful to use pictures or images, to let a child draw their own pictures, or to observe them in their play. It is especially useful to watch children playing with clay or play-dough, because these mediums are excellent materials for allowing children to release their feelings such as anger or frustration, both of which can be difficult to express verbally.

Step 2
Acknowledge the feelings of the child and listen carefully to their views and opinions.

Ask a child to tell or show you how they feel, and to explain to you or show you why they are behaving in certain ways. Take your cues from the child and try not to probe if they are reluctant to express themselves. Remember younger children may struggle to express how they feel. Again, observe and watch the child and use this information to help you help the child.

Step 3
Explain to the child why you find their behaviour unacceptable, or how it may hurt or upset others.

Match your explanation to the stage and level of development. Older children may be able to understand the consequences of their actions, for example, you could say, 'If you don't play this game by the rules, the other children will become upset', or 'If you continue to kick the football indoors, you may break a window and the club will have to pay for the repairs rather than buy more equipment'. Younger children may not yet be able to understand the impact of their actions on others, so it might be better to appeal to their need for security and safety by saying something like, 'if you climb onto the table, you might fall off and really hurt yourself.'

Hannah was the officer-in-charge in the pre-school room of a large day nursery. One of the boys, Josh, was causing concern to staff and other children. He had frequently shouted angrily at other children using inappropriate language and was easily distracted. Hannah wanted to find out if anything was bothering the child and tried talking to him quietly after lunch. She also made an appointment to speak to the boy's mother about her concerns. Josh told Hannah that Mummy and Daddy often shouted at each other and he didn't like it. Hannah asked Josh what it was he didn't like and how he felt. He said that he felt scared when they shouted and it made him cry. Hannah tried to explain to Josh that when he shouted the other children didn't like it and that she wanted to help him to learn not to shout. Hannah told Josh's mother about her conversation with Josh and how he was feeling. Mum admitted that she and her partner were having problems, but had not realised the effect that this was having on Josh. Hannah decided that if Josh's attention span could be increased he would find fewer opportunities to shout at other children. Staff agreed that they would focus their strategy on increasing Josh's attention span. They decided to play more small group games and activities alongside and with him, read stories in small groups (rather than as a class), and make sure that at snack and meal times, Josh sat next to an adult.

This strategy was based on the social learning theory, with other children and adults being positive role models.

Empowering the child

As discussed in Part 1, empowerment is about helping children to develop confidence and positive self-esteem so that they are able to manage their own behaviour. To do this effectively we must listen carefully at all times to what children are telling us, not just through their words, but also through their actions, facial expressions and body language. We need to know what they need and want.

The main focus of empowerment is to give children opportunities where they are in control of situations. This strategy can be introduced and developed with young children by offering them opportunities to make choices; for example, a child could be asked, 'Do you want milk or water to drink?' or, 'Do you want to play with the cars on the floor or at the table?' Older children can be encouraged to make more complex decisions involving deciding between several things, such as which television programmes to watch or to video.

Some early years workers find that giving children specific responsibilities can help them to feel empowered, provided that the tasks are manageable.

When a child carries out their tasks of responsibility they feel inwardly rewarded and motivated. Not only does this make them feel empowered but also helps to build up self-confidence and self-esteem.

CASE STUDY

A pre-school group provides children with a drink and something to eat halfway through each session. One of the staff makes enough toast for each child to have one piece and pours two different drinks into jugs. At break time the children sit at tables, in small groups with their key worker. Each child is given a plate, a beaker and two knives. The children are asked to decide if they want juice or water to drink; sometimes the choice might be milk or water, or juice and milk. They are then asked if they want to spread their toast with a 'butter' spread and finally if they want cheese spread or Marmite; sometimes the choice might be honey or cheese spread, or honey and peanut butter. The staff take into consideration the individual dietary needs of the children, but try to offer at least two opportunities during break time to allow the children to make choices and learn decision-making skills. They have found that the behaviour of all of the children is appropriate during this time, even though break time can take much longer than it did when children were just presented with a drink and toast. At the end of break time, one child from each group has the responsibility for collecting the beakers, knives and plates and taking them to the hatchway into the kitchen, where a member of staff washes up.

1 Suggest two ways in which this pre-school group is empowering children.

2 Why do you think the behaviour of all of the children is described by the staff as 'appropriate' during break time?

The children's charity Kidscape has developed excellent programmes and strategies to empower children who are being bullied or abused. Many of these work on the basis of building and developing confidence and communication skills. Children are encouraged to learn ways of keeping themselves safe through playing games such as *'What would do if you got lost?'* or *''What would you do if someone asked you to keep a secret?'* Such games put the child in control, coming up with solutions or suggestions and deciding on strategies. Played with a sensitive adult, games such as these can give children confidence and build self-esteem. These strategies can equally be used with children who display unwanted or inappropriate behaviour by encouraging them to consider hypothetical scenarios.

Amir, aged six, frequently made unnecessary noises, such as banging objects, scraping chairs, or moving around the classroom deliberately and clumsily to create a noise. His teacher had tried asking him not to do this, but this strategy had not worked and the teacher felt that she was in danger of always 'nagging' Amir. The teacher decided that the class would play 'What if' or 'What would happen if' games at the end of the day and that she would gradually introduce questions along the lines of, 'What would happen if we all scraped our chairs at the same time?' or 'What if I knocked someone over because I wasn't careful about how I moved around our room?' The teacher made sure that none of the questions was directed at Amir and that all of the children had the opportunity to suggest a 'what if' question. Some of the children suggested questions that were not related to behaviour at all but still positively contributed to the discussion. This reinforced the strategy of enabling children to make choices and decisions. This game improved communication skills, both speaking and listening. The teacher noticed that initially Amir did not participate freely; he neither suggested a question, nor gave a possible answer. The first time he did contribute, both the teacher and the other children praised him. Gradually Amir began to participate more, and as his participation in the game increased, the incidences of inappropriate behaviour decreased.

Acknowledge the feelings of the child

All children have feelings that are both positive and negative. Sometimes a child's feelings can be very strong and powerful, such as excitement, anger, fear or jealousy. It can be that in certain situations a child does not have the language or communication skills to tell us how they are feeling and so they may express themselves in actions and behaviour. Sometimes children show negative feelings because they do not feel that they are in control, for example, children can be jealous of a new baby in the family and angry with the parents for not giving them as much attention as before. Look again at the snapshot of Hannah and Josh (page 108). Think about how Hannah found out how Josh was feeling, before she decided on a strategy. This shows that she respected and acknowledged Josh's feelings and took his worries and concerns very seriously. She did not probe or delve into why his parents were shouting; she focused on Josh and his feelings and concerns.

A child's feelings are very real and should not be dismissed lightly. We must recognise a child's feelings and help them to express them and, if appropriate, learn how to control them. Giving our full attention when children are speaking or communicating to us, listening attentively and having good eye contact can achieve this. We must make sure that our body language does not give different messages to what we are saying. For example, standing with our arms folded can be interpreted as being impatient and wanting to get on and do something else, when our words might be saying, 'why don't we talk about how you are feeling'. It would be better to get down to the same physical level as the child, perhaps by sitting together on the floor, or kneeling. This would also improve our eye contact with the child.

We must acknowledge and respond to all types of feelings. When children express negative feelings, such as anger, we often focus on those feelings and forget to acknowledge children when they are happy.

Be clear about priorities

We should try to have a reasonably sound idea of our aims and objectives in managing children's behaviour. Managing behaviour should be regarded as a means to an end, not an end in itself. It is important to remember that adults, as well as children, have a right to have their needs considered, and that adult and child relationships need to be balanced.

The late child psychologist **Dr Haim Ginott** (1924–1974) suggested that adults should consider children's behaviour as falling into three colour codes – green, amber and red – like traffic lights. By following this coding of behaviour, it is possible to clarify our aims and objectives: the types of behaviour that we want to encourage, those that we will tolerate and those that we want to change.

Green

This is the 'go-ahead' type of behaviour that adults approve of from children, such as sharing toys with one another, eating a meal without a fuss and sitting attentively listening to a story. Green behaviours should be encouraged and praised. They include individual attributes of the child – aspects of their personality which make them unique.

Amber

This is the 'caution' behaviour, which is not actively encouraged but may be tolerated, because the child is still learning and making mistakes. This might include 'decorating' the bedroom walls with finger paints or felt pens, throwing toys across the room in a moment of frustration and anger. Any sort of stress or upset may lead to a temporary regression in behaviour, such as wetting the bed; this would be regarded as amber behaviour.

Red

This is the definite 'stop' behaviour, which needs to be curbed as soon as possible. Often red behaviours can cause harm or injury to the child or others, such as running out into the road, touching a hot object, or biting and scratching another child.

Encourage bonds of respect and affections

The more respect and affection that there is between an adult and a child, the easier it is to reach an agreement over behaviour. If there is unacceptable behaviour, it should be very clear to a child that the adult, whether parent or carer, disapproves of their *actions* not the child him- or herself. It is not positive to say, 'You've been very naughty, I don't love you any more.' This implies that affection and love are conditional and that the adult disapproves of the child as a whole. It is far more positive to make sure that remarks specifically address the behaviour or actions, for example, 'I don't like it when you hit other children.'

CASE STUDY

Sam is four years old and attends a nursery class attached to the local primary school five mornings a week. He is due to start school next term. Sam's mum has been told by one of the nursery staff that he is a problem at story time and circle time because he won't sit still and listen; he constantly interrupts and distracts the other children. The staff member tells Sam's mum that she told him that the 'big' school teacher won't want him in her class if he doesn't sit still and that she won't like him.

1 What might have been a better way for the nursery staff to have spoken to Sam?

2 What might Sam now think about his next teacher? Why?

3 What would you do in a similar situation?

Set limits

Setting limits is about establishing an acceptable framework. When establishing a framework, the main concern should be for a child's safety, well-being and overall development. Rules should not be made for the sake of having rules. For example, it is in the best interests of all children that accidents within a school environment are prevented as much as possible; therefore a school rule, or set limit, might be that children must walk at all times in corridors, or that children must walk on the right-hand side of corridors or stairs, regardless of which direction they are moving in. The school might also set a limit which states that there should be no running in corridors. This is, however, focusing on a negative action – do not run – rather than a positive action – everyone should walk.

When setting limits or establishing a framework, ask yourself the following questions:

1 **Are the rules fair?** Do both adults and children regard the rules as fair? For example, is it fair that children in a day-care setting are not allowed to put their feet on the furniture if they see the staff putting their feet on chairs during their breaks?

2 **Are the rules simple?** It is easier to remember simple rules, such as, 'Inside we walk everywhere,' rather than, 'We do not run around the nursery rooms, hallway and toilets.'

3 **Does the child understand the rules?** Is the language you use to tell children about the framework or rules appropriate to their stage of development? Is the concept behind the rule or framework one that children have the intellectual maturity to understand?

4 **Does the child know and understand what will happen if the rules are broken?** Children at certain stages of their cognitive development cannot understand the consequences of their actions. There is little point in saying to a child, 'You must not go into the kitchen on your own as you could hurt yourself.' It might be better to say, 'I want to make sure that you and all of the other children are safe. There are things in the kitchen that could hurt you, such as the oven. I do not want any child to be hurt, so we will all go into the kitchen together, then we can make sure that we are all safe.'

5 **Are the rules applied consistently?** Children should be able to see clearly that the rule or framework applies to everyone in that setting and in the same way. There is little point in having a rule about sitting down at story time, if one childcare worker enforces the rule, but another does not. The children will quickly learn that one member of staff treats them differently, and may interpret this inconsistency as someone not really caring about them as they can't be bothered to stick to the same rules as everyone else.

6 **Do your rules and framework reflect the standards of your community, religion, values or life style?** If your rules or limits do not reflect these standards, you may find it difficult to adhere to them. You may feel as if you are going against the things that you believe and may not, therefore, feel committed.

Be consistent

It important to be consistent – especially when we are aiming to help children distinguish between appropriate and inappropriate behaviour. Not only does inconsistency give out the message that some adults do not care as much as others, but it is also confusing. A child will become very confused if they are reprimanded for the way they behave today, but tomorrow they get away with the same behaviour. Being consistent is not easy. For example, adults often hold out against children's demands for some time, but eventually give in for a variety of reasons. It may be that the child has pleaded and whined to the point where the adult is exhausted and irritable and so gives in for a bit of peace and quiet. By doing this the child has learnt that if they make enough fuss, one way or another they will get what they want.

An adult who is consistent reassures a child's need for security – they know what the framework and rules are. However, this does not mean that the adult has to be rigid and inflexible. Children change as they mature, situations change, and childcare workers and parents may change, especially in their understanding of children. Responsible and professional adults must be prepared to adapt and modify their framework and rules to meet new circumstances, but adults should always discuss these proposed changes with children.

ACTIVITY

Genna, aged six, wants a packet of crisps; she asks her childminder if she can have some. The childminder replies that it is nearly time for her meal and that she can't have any crisps, and that she didn't say please either. Genna is not satisfied with this response and continues to ask, using a 'whingy' voice and still not saying please. The childminder continues to say no and does not give in to Genna's demands. Genna gets very cross and shouts, 'I hate you.' She then starts to cry and repeatedly makes the same demand, using the same tone of voice and not saying please. Eventually the childminder gives in and Genna is given the crisps.

1   What mixed messages could Genna be getting from the situation described above?

2   How do you think the childminder should respond to Genna's outburst of, 'I hate you'?

3   How could this situation have been avoided?

It is one thing to be totally consistent over vital principles of behaviour, for example, things that affect a child's safety, such as crossing a road, but it is another to be unrelenting in response to every incident. If a childminder and child have agreed a fixed bedtime, it does not necessarily mean that the childminder is being inconsistent to allow the child to stay up later occasionally. Similarly, since adults need to 'let off steam' and vent their feelings every now and then, it should be acceptable to let a child do the same.

Focus on the positive things

For many children the need to seek attention is one of the main reasons why they behave in inappropriate ways. If behaving in an unacceptable way gains an adult's attention, even if it is only to be told to stop doing something, a child has achieved their goal. Sometimes the child's need for attention is far greater than the fear of getting into trouble, and if behaving in such a way causes the adult to respond in a negative way, then negative attention is better than no attention at all. Often adults forget to respond to acceptable or 'good' behaviour. Children who are playing well together may appear to need little adult intervention in the form of praise; however, when a dispute or argument starts, the adult does start to pay more attention. It is important therefore to praise positive behaviour.

> **ACTIVITY**
>
> Focusing on positive things – explaining to them what they *can* do rather than what they cannot – gives a more favourable message to children. Below are a few rules that many childcare and educational professionals use. Note that they have been deliberately written to focus on something negative. Read each one and then in the space alongside, try to write a more positive rule.
>
> | Negative 'rule' | Positive 'rule' |
> | --- | --- |
> | Don't pick rubbish up off the ground. | |
> | Don't leave those toys out. | |
> | Don't hit other children. | |
> | Don't draw on the walls. | |
> | Don't push other children. | |

Focusing on positive things is also about offering 'rewards' for appropriate actions and behaviour. It is very important that the attention or focus that the adult gives is considered and thoughtful. If every time we walk past a group of children playing and sharing well, we say, 'That's good', these children will eventually ignore us and our comment will be meaningless, even though it is positive. We have to remember to give adequate and quality attention to each and every child. The term 'quality time' has slipped into common usage and is often much maligned. However, spending a few minutes with a child to talk about positive things they have been doing is far more beneficial than spending all day saying, 'Don't do that' or 'No!'

THINK IT OVER:

What sort of day have you had with the children in your care today? Good, bad or average?

Think about one child in your care whose behaviour at times you find challenging. How many times today have you focused on the positive things that the child has done, and told them? How many times did you find yourself using negative language to manage the child's behaviour?

The next time you are working with the child try to make a conscious effort to accentuate the positive things that the child does, no matter how seemingly small or insignificant, and talk about these things with the child.

Give clear explanations

Giving explanations is essential to a child's development. They enable a child to learn more about their world. Explanations help children to begin to understand the effects of their behaviour. Simply saying to a child, 'You are a very naughty girl,' without any other explanation, does not help the child to understand what they have done or why it was wrong.

Explanations are more effective when children are developmentally mature enough to understand the consequences of their actions. For example, older children may only need to be made aware of the effect of their behaviour on others, or the possible dangers that they could cause for themselves or others, to change their behaviour.

THINK IT OVER:

Many adults do not unquestioningly obey rules without finding out the reasons for them, yet they may expect children to obey rules without question. Ask yourself: if your work place introduced a 'dress casually on Fridays' rule or banned staff car parking, would you accept this without question? Surely you and your colleagues would start to ask questions about who decided this, why you weren't consulted and how this might affect you personally?

Explanations may also be effective when describing possible sanctions or punishments in the event of unwanted behaviour continuing; for example, we could say to a child, 'If you continue throwing the ball at the window I will take it away from you.' However, children are more likely to internalise standards of acceptable behaviour if these are justified and explained in terms of their fundamental value, i.e. why they are important, rather than in terms of the punishments or reprimands that follow disobedience. Consider the following exchange between childcare worker (CCW) and Anya (A), aged four:

CCW You mustn't do that!

A Why not?

CCW Because you mustn't.

A But why mustn't I?

CCW Because it is wrong.

A But why is it wrong?

CCW Because I say so! Now that's enough, go and play with Timi.

All children need to know *why*. The exchange above gives Anya no explanation as to why what she was doing was wrong, so Anya has not learnt any new skills or gained any new knowledge, other than how to get the attention of the childcare worker. It is important that Anya understands why something she did was wrong. If she understands this, it is more likely that she will not do it again. A more acceptable exchange, which is more beneficial to Anya and the childcare worker, could have gone something along the lines of:

CCW You mustn't do that!

A Why not?

CCW Because you might hurt yourself.

A Why might I hurt myself?

CCW Because you could fall off the back of the chair and bang your head on the floor, or on the edge of the table.

A What would happen then?

CCW You could get a big lump on your head, or even a nasty cut. You could have a bad headache after banging your head and we might have to take you to see a doctor.

Conversations like the first one often happen at the end of a busy working day, when both the childcare worker and the children are tired and patience is not at the level it might have been first thing in the morning. Replying to Anya as in the second conversation does take more thought and possibly time, but is more beneficial in the long run.

Listen

Listening is a fundamental part of communication. It is not a passive activity. Active listening is essential if we are to fully understand the children in our care. Children's communications are often in 'code'. They may say one thing and mean something else. Children may have special words for certain actions, such as going to the toilet, or use gestures and body language that seem to be giving us a different message from what they are saying. It is our job to de-code children's communications. Adults need to show empathy, listening to what children say with one ear tuned into what they are *not* saying – the hidden messages. For example, a child who comes home from school and declares, 'I hate school' is not really saying that he or she hates *everything* about school, but might be saying, 'I feel embarrassed when getting changed for P.E. because I am very slow at getting dressed', or 'I don't understand what the teacher is saying because I can't hear very well'. Listening attentively to what a child is saying helps them to express themselves as they know that we are really taking in what they are saying and that we also respect and acknowledge their views and opinions.

SNAPSHOT

Katrina, eight years old, kept telling her childminder that she was fine and that there was nothing wrong when she stopped playing with the other children after school and wanted to sit by herself and watch television. Her childminder persisted with trying to talk to Katrina, despite her assurances that she was OK. The childminder could tell from Katrina's body language that something was wrong. It turned out that Katrina was being bullied at school and didn't know how to talk about it as she felt ashamed and frightened.

Making eye contact is an important part of listening and communication with children

Being a good listener and understanding the hidden messages that children are sending requires time, effort and concentration. Being an effective listener does not come naturally to some people; they find that they are easily distracted, or that their feelings about an individual affects how well they listen. There are definite things that you can do to help them listen to children more effectively:

◆ Give a child your undivided attention.

◆ Ask open-ended questions to show that you have listened, that you want more information or to clarify something that you may not have heard correctly; for example, a child that tells you that they were kept in by their teacher might prompt the response, 'That must have upset you. Would you like to tell me what happened?'

◆ Summarise what has been said. This makes you listen carefully, lets the child who was speaking know that you have understood what they were saying and reduces the possibility of misunderstanding.

◆ Let a child know that you are listening carefully. Maintain eye contact, use appropriate gestures and body language, such as nods of your head and perhaps saying words like 'mmm' or 'yes'.

Use praise and encouragement (positive reinforcement)

In Part 1, the behaviourist theories of Skinner and Thorndike were discussed in terms of rewarding behaviours that were acceptable. Both Skinner and Thorndike worked with animals to develop their theories, but they also applied the theory to children. Rewarding a child with praise, encouragement and attention is likely to result in the child repeating that action. Taking this theory further, if we wish to encourage a child to be kind and thoughtful towards others, we should tell the child how pleased we are every time we see them sharing toys or comforting a distressed child. Once the child has acquired this form of behaviour, we need only reward the child occasionally to reinforce their good behaviour.

SNAPSHOT

Maggie minds two children after school as well as her own son. Her son shows signs of jealousy when the two other children are around and is very reluctant to let them play with some of his toys. When the children come in from school Maggie gives them a snack and usually lets the children watch a short video or listen to a story tape.

To try to manage her son's jealousy Maggie also talks to her son about the problem, and asks him what he feels he can happily share with the other children. Her son felt that he would be willing to share his Lego set. Maggie praises him for letting the other two children play with his Lego. Maggie does this every day for three weeks, during which time she notices that her son has gradually let the others play with his paint set. During the fourth week Maggie sticks to her routine, but does not praise her son every time the children watch a video or listen to tapes. She also begins to praise him when all the children are playing together. Her son gradually becomes less jealous of the other children and more willing to share and co-operate. Maggie continues to praise her son occasionally to reinforce his appropriate behaviour towards the other children.

Some adults see giving rewards in any shape or form, including praise and encouragement, as a form of bribery, for example, encouraging a child to work hard and pass an examination with the promise of a special treat if they are successful. This raises an ethical question – is it appropriate to offer children rewards for passing examinations or tests? In all probability, in such cases we are trying to encourage the child to put in more effort. If the child is not successful in the tests or examination, despite trying, we are placed in a difficult position because it was the effort that they were initially trying to encourage (and the child did try), but the reward was for the result. Parents might consider offering a reward for effort instead. In addition, bribery is actually a reward for corrupt or dishonest actions, whereas reward in this context should be seen as treats or privileges. The person who has lost a few kilos in weight will give themselves a treat, in the same way that an individual who has successfully given up smoking for a month will reward themselves with something special. This is not bribery.

Rewards may take many forms as well as praise and encouragement. Attention may be a valuable reward, as may a smile or words of thanks and appreciation. To be effective, rewards should not be handed out freely or without thought. We should be very clear in our own minds as to what exactly we are trying to encourage and reward. A child's actions are influenced by much more than the particular nature of the reward. The child must also understand the relationship between their own action and behaviour, and the reward.

CASE STUDY

Five-year-old Afoluka always caused a scene and sulked if the classroom assistant did not let her hand round the drinks at snack time. Sometimes the assistant would give in to Afoluka and let her do it, just to keep the peace, but the other children began to object, saying that it was not fair to let Afoluka have this 'important' job when she was not behaving properly. The classroom assistant and Afoluka talked about her unacceptable behaviour and how it was affecting other children. They decided that Afoluka could hand out the drinks on a Friday, but only if she did not cause a scene or sulk on the other days of the week when other children did the job. To reinforce this decision, Afoluka and the assistant made a simple chart that recorded with smiley or sad faces how Afoluka had reacted at snack time. If Afoluka had four smiley faces by Friday, she handed round the drinks; if she had not got four, another child was chosen.

1 What do you think about this situation?
2 Was this a fair and consistent way to handle Afoluka's inappropriate behaviour?
3 What was the reward?
4 Do you think it would work?
5 If not, why not? What would you do in similar circumstances?

A calm environment

Most people would agree that life today is far more stressful, hectic, pressurised and busy than it was for the last generation. Carers who are under pressure and stress can sometimes, unwittingly, transfer their stressful feelings to their children. In some cases, the early years setting or school can be one of the few places that a child can relax and unwind. Early years settings and school are often busy environments, but can still be places of calm. Voices do not need to be raised; children and staff can speak to one another calmly, even when dealing with minor disagreements and arguments. It should not ever be necessary to shout; an adult who shouts, teaches children to shout.

It is possible to arrange the play or classroom environment so that one area is designated a quiet zone. Children may want to look at or read books, play a quiet game, or just sit and watch others. Everyone needs a place where they can be quiet and sometimes be on their own. Many adults use the drive home from work as their quiet time to unwind and listen to their favourite music. We all need time to take in what has happened to us, give our brains a chance to sort out this information and decide what we are going to do with it, or, in Piagetian terms, assimilate and accommodate it.

ACTIVITY

Think about the layout of your work setting. Make a rough plan of how the room or areas are organised. Then ask yourself the following questions:

◆ Is it obvious, both to children and adults in your work environment, that there are designated areas for specific activities? For example, many early years settings have a book and reading area, or an area specifically set aside for messy play because it is near a sink.

◆ Does the way that your work setting is organised allow for free movement around the area, or are there obstacles? For example, can children move easily between the messy play area and the place where they will wash their hands, and is the book area set apart so that it is not a thoroughfare to another area?

◆ Has your workplace got a specifically designated area where children, and adults, can be quiet, an area that is not a thoroughfare to another place, an area where children and adults can just sit and contemplate and watch others?

◆ If you answered *no* to the above question, in particular, can you think of ways that you could rearrange your working environment so that there is a really quiet and calm area?

There is a tendency in some day nurseries and childcare settings for every moment of the day to be filled with activity, hustle and bustle, with children having very little time to be quiet, watch, observe and contemplate the activities and actions of others. Some staff believe that if the children are inactive, they are not doing anything worthwhile, but this is far from true!

Using colours to create a calm environment

Colours may play a significant part in creating a calm environment. It is well known that blue, green and some pastel shades may be calming and relaxing, whereas red, yellow and orange may be stimulating. Many early years establishments deliberately decorate the place in bright stimulating colours, to make the rooms look inviting and interesting places to learn, which is very commendable. At the same time, however, it is important to be aware of the effect of colour on some children, and childcare settings should consider the use of more relaxing and calming colours in some areas where children can relax, unwind and be quiet and calm. How can we realistically expect a child who is agitated and perhaps distressed to calm down and relax when they are surrounded by bright, stimulating colours?

CASE STUDY

Milly, aged three years, attends a day nursery from 8 am to 6 pm every weekday. The nursery is busy and prides itself on the wide range of stimulating activities that it plans and provides for all of the children. The prospectus for parents emphasises that 'We make sure that your child will be kept fully occupied all the time that they are in our care.' The nursery is brightly decorated throughout and staff believe that they have created a positive environment in which to care for children. However, in the afternoons Milly often has 'temper tantrums', especially when she can't get her own way, and becomes agitated. Staff have noticed that Milly, and several other children, become cross and aggressive towards each other and that some behaviour is becoming difficult to manage. When staff seek advice from their local early years mentor as to the best way to deal with Milly's behaviour, it is suggested that they need to look again at the routine of the day and how they speak to the children.

1 Why do you think the mentor suggested that the nursery look at their routine?

2 Why do you think the mentor asked the nursery staff to think about how they speak to the children?

3 Why do you think Milly and the other children could be displaying unwanted behaviour?

4 What would you do in such circumstances?

Distractions

The effectiveness of some strategies depends on the age of the children. For example, time-out (see page 124) is more effective with older children, while distraction is more effective with younger children. The intention is to manage

Distraction can be an effective strategy to discourage inappropriate behaviour

the unwanted behaviour by distracting or by drawing attention to something else. For example, if a young child wants a toy that another child is already playing with, they might be appeased by being offered another toy to play with.

Sometimes distraction can be an effective strategy to use to try to stop a child engaging in comfort behaviour, such as masturbation, nail biting or thumb-sucking. By focusing too obviously on the comfort behaviour, the adult may actually reinforce the behaviour that they wish to eliminate, so every time the child puts his or her thumb in their mouth, they are distracted, by being given an activity to do, or something else to occupy the hands. If a child's hands are occupied with some interesting activity, he or she cannot engage in comfort behaviour at the same time. This is a form of behaviour modification.

Facial expression and body language

Many adults who work with children have a 'talent' for being able to control children by just giving them a 'look' or just simply by being there and aware of the child. One of the main benefits of this strategy is that it shows the child that you are calm and in control of the situation. Words are usually not necessary. Disapproval can be shown by particular facial expressions or stances; these have to be genuine or else children will 'see straight through' them and there is the danger that the expression or stance will not be taken seriously. Usually, once the child is aware that the adult disapproves of their behaviour and is unhappy, they will begin to behave in more appropriate ways. At this point, facial expressions should convey pleasure and approval. This strategy often works effectively for relatively minor misdemeanours, such as talking in class.

CASE STUDY

Brenda was a very experienced Key Stage 1 teacher who had a very quiet voice. She had taught at the same school for many years and no one had ever heard her raise her voice at any time. Over the years she taught many children who had difficulty managing their behaviour. She only had to look at a child to let them know that she did not approve of their actions and similarly her ready smile was reward enough for many children who managed their behaviour in a positive way.

1 Have you ever met anyone like Brenda?

2 How did they use body language or facial expressions to guide and help children?

3 If you use this strategy, think about when you use it and for what reasons.

Saying 'No!'

The golden rule for this strategy is to use it carefully; if it is used too frequently, the seriousness of the message will be lost. Like other strategies, if the word 'No' is used inconsistently it will cease to be effective. It becomes more effective if the person saying 'No' maintains eye contact with the child. There are times when carers will say that 'No' is the most common word that they use with a young child. Distraction is often a more effective strategy to use than continually saying 'No'.

THINK IT OVER:

Moshi, aged two, was visiting an antique shop with his childminder. The shop had many ornaments and 'knick-knacks'. He walked around the room pointing at the objects and saying 'that's a no, that's a no.' On a previous visit his childminder had said 'No' every time Moshi touched an ornament.

Do you think Moshi understood what 'No' really meant or do you think that he had learnt that the ornaments were called 'No'?

Which theory could explain how Moshi is learning?

Time-out

This strategy could be described as a disarming strategy as it allows the adult, once the child has been removed, to create a more harmonious atmosphere. It allows both the child and the adult to compose themselves and calm down. This strategy usually works more effectively with older children, who often respond more positively to being removed from a situation that is causing them difficulties.

Time-out should not be used as a sanction or punishment, or children are likely to feel rejected and excluded. This could increase the possibility of further problems in the future. No child should ever be left on their own, unsupervised or unattended, but can be sat or moved away from other children. This creates a physical sense of space between them and gives the child a sense of their own 'space'.

CASE STUDY

One primary school decided to use 'time-out' with a slight difference as a way of managing children's behaviour at lunchtimes. The lunchtime supervisors were having numerous problems with children behaving in inappropriate ways and they found that they were spending much of their time dealing with problems rather than actually playing with or positively interacting with the children. As the football World Cup was due to take place the staff, teachers and lunchtime supervisors decided that the time-out would have a football theme. They thought that the children might be more responsive, which would make the strategy more effective, and decided to try it for half a term. A child who behaved in an inappropriate way at lunchtime was shown a yellow card and asked to sit on a bench. The supervisors took it in turns to 'man' the bench and record the names of the children who had received a yellow card. After ten minutes the children were allowed to go back to the play area. If a child received three yellow cards in one week or did something that put other children at risk, or used violent and aggressive language towards an adult, they were given a red card and immediately sent to the head teacher. It became apparent after only two weeks that several children had responded well to the yellow card system and that the incidences of inappropriate behaviour had decreased. This strategy was not effective for all of the children who behaved in inappropriate ways, but as it had been helpful for others it was continued.

1 Give two reasons why this use of 'time-out' was not effective for all of the children.

2 Can you think of any disadvantages to this way of managing the children's behaviour?

Removal of equipment

In some ways the removal of equipment is rather like time-out, in that it deprives a child of something that they want, in this case equipment and toys. However, many people believe that the removal of toys or equipment should only be used as a final resort and only when children are in danger of hurting themselves or others. It is very important to explain to children why the toy or piece of equipment is being removed.

THINK IT OVER:

Sally and Thomas are arguing about which television programme to watch and cannot be pacified. Mike, their father, switches off the television so neither child can get what they want.

What have the children actually learnt from this situation? Has Sally and Thomas's attention-seeking behaviour succeeded?

What have Sally and Thomas learnt about adults in this scenario?

Can you think how else this situation might have been resolved?

Play therapy

Play, in all of its many forms, should be a source of fun, relaxation and enjoyment. There are many adults who go to a gym or swimming pool after a day's work in order to work out their tensions and stresses. In many respects this is a form of relaxation and therapy, and should be fun; it can be seen as an adult form of play. In the same way, play can help children work out tensions and stresses that may be causing them to behave in certain ways.

Children are usually referred to play therapists by other professionals, such as health visitors or educational psychologists. Play therapy is closely linked to the psychoanalytical theories of Freud, and is another branch of psychoanalysis – a method of treating adults with psychological difficulties and disorders. Psychoanalysis involves helping an individual to become aware of unconscious feelings and emotions that may have affected their actions and behaviour, and it involves a lot of intensive talking. Play therapists use play therapy rather than psychoanalysis to help children express unconscious feelings and emotions, because many children have not yet developed the necessary range of verbal and other communication skills to express themselves. Psychoanalysts and play therapists believe that causes of 'problems' can be found in the unconscious mind, and that once a child has understood what has caused a 'problem' or incident of inappropriate behaviour, the behaviour will disappear.

A skilled play therapist will gain insight into a child's feelings and behavioural patterns through watching, observing and listening as they play. It is quite usual practice for a play therapist to use a two-way mirror to observe a child playing. Once the therapist is aware of, and understands the child's feelings, they can help him or her to recognise these feelings and together develop strategies to deal with them.

Play therapists also use play as a diagnostic tool, as they observe, listen and watch children at play. Diagnoses can be made about the reasons why a child is behaving in certain ways and perhaps other professionals can be made aware of related problems, for example, a medical condition. Hospital play specialists may use play therapy to help a child overcome fears about their bodies or medical procedures.

One of the arguments against play theory, particularly for managing behaviour and empowering children, is that it might only work with children who are young enough to play with toys, and is therefore not an appropriate strategy for older children.

Play therapy can help children to express their emotions and deal with difficult situations

The benefits of role-play

Play may take the fear out of a situation and thereby act as a form of therapy and healing. For children, play can and does provide good opportunities to act out situations that could cause anxiety and potentially lead to problems with their behaviour. It is quite common practice to set up a role-play area as a hospital when early years workers become aware that a child or family member may be going into hospital. This type of play helps children to express some of their fears and concerns in a familiar, non-threatening environment. Role-play or drama can be a very effective strategy to help children act out significant experiences.

CASE STUDY

A teacher in a large primary school uses role-play to help the children in his year 4 class learn about and deal with a wide range of social situations. For example, he uses role-play to help children learn appropriate responses if they feel that their safety is threatened, or how to respond to a bully, or what to do if someone offers them a cigarette, alcohol or drugs. The teacher also uses role-play to help the children see situations from another person's point of view and so develop a greater understanding of how others may be feeling. These role-play sessions happen about twice a week and often last only about 10 minutes, at most. The sessions are introduced through a brief open-ended question and answer session and end with the class discussing some of the issues raised. The teacher finds these activities very worthwhile and beneficial to all of the children. He does not expect every child to participate in the actual role-play but does expect every child to take part in the introduction and discussions. He has found that the children respond very positively to the role-play and often suggest scenarios themselves.

1   Could you do something along these lines in your work setting?
2   Perhaps you are already using role-play in this way. Can you think of any ways that you might extend it to help manage aspects of children's behaviour?

Most children naturally play in an imaginative way and this can be used by sensitive adults to help manage their behaviour. Play situations can be created whereby a toy or imaginary character behaves in an inappropriate way. In the play session the child is encouraged to think about the scenario and act out the possible consequences of the behaviour. Many adults have found this a useful strategy to help children understand some of the consequences of their actions and the feelings of others.

Play can provide children with opportunities to express strong emotions in a safe and secure way. If a child is angry, cross or frustrated, it is far better to let them take out their anger and possible aggression in a play activity rather than on another child. This is where physical or vigorous play can help a child release emotions, use up surplus energy and help to dissipate anger and frustrations. Play-dough and soft apparatus can also be used in play therapies.

Sometimes children who lack self-confidence, or have poor communication skills, find it very difficult to put their feelings into words and may therefore display inappropriate behaviours in attempting to express themselves. Sometimes feelings can be expressed through paintings, drawings and other tactile activities. Many professionals who work with children who have been abused use small-scale toys, puppets and dolls in play situations to help children express themselves and explain their experiences.

Music

Many children with behavioural and/or emotional difficulties respond positively to music. Music can have a very calming influence and has universal appeal. This appeal is possibly associated with the rhythmic nature of music and the link with nature's body rhythms, such as a heartbeat. It has been shown that listening to tape recordings of the mother's regular heartbeat sometimes calms babies who are difficult to soothe and settle. This 'music' is what an unborn child hears whilst in the mother's womb and these sounds and rhythms are often referred to as 'womb music'. The rhythms of music and melodies often reflect natural rhythms and inflections of conversations, and so being given the opportunity to respond to music may help a child with communication difficulties. Therapists can use different types of music with different children, for example, calming quiet music may soothe a restless child, while loud, powerful music may help a child express strong and powerful emotions.

Playing instruments may help children release and express feelings and emotions, but in a controlled manner. Often this form of play therapy takes place in small group situations and this helps children develop social skills. Children need to listen to one another, respond to the cues of others and take turns. Exposure to music from different cultures may help to create respect for these cultures and may also boost the self-esteem of children in the early years setting who come from that culture.

Children can enjoy making music as well as listening to it

THINK IT OVER:

◆ Take your cues from a child, for example, give the child a drum, wait for them to make a sound from it, then reply to the child, either by copying what they did or by adding a complementary rhythm. (This also has the benefit of allowing the child to make the first move, take responsibility and therefore be empowered.)

◆ Sing a short tune, or clap a rhythm, and then ask children to repeat what you did. This will encourage concentration and listening skills. Extend this activity by asking a child to clap a rhythm or sing a short tune which is then repeated by the rest of the group, including yourself. This helps empower a child.

◆ Play quiet, soothing music, such as pan pipes or a single instrument, when children appear to be stressed or when you want them to relax.

◆ Play lively music, such as orchestral or big band music, marches, vigorous dance music, etc. when you want children to tidy up or move to another activity. Used in this way music can be an alternative to voice commands, and children quickly learn what they are expected to do when they hear different styles of music.

Non-effective strategies

Whilst we should always aim to use positive and effective strategies to empower and guide children there are some strategies that are still used, but that could be described as negative and damaging to children. It is important that we understand these strategies as well, because it helps us to understand the benefits of using positive ways to guide and empower children.

Smacking

Smacking was discussed in Chapter 5, and the debate for and against smacking still continues. It is not out of the ordinary to see adults smack or hit children in public places, such as shopping centres or supermarkets. Many people express the view that a smack is short, sharp, instant negative reinforcement (Skinner's theory). However, often a smack is accompanied by raised voices and strong emotions and feelings, which can complicate the messages being received by a child.

There are many alternative strategies to smacking, such as distracting the child or giving a clear explanation of why the behaviour or action is inappropriate or unacceptable, and why the adult feels angry or cross. Many of these strategies have already been discussed in this chapter.

> ## CASE STUDY
>
> Janie's parents have smacked her from babyhood. They believe that smacking has taught Janie, now six, right from wrong. In the pre-school group the staff noticed that Janie would smack the dolls in the role-play area and tell them they were very naughty. In the reception class the teacher noticed that Janie would occasionally hit other children when they did something that she considered to be 'naughty', such as messing about in the toilets.
>
> 1 Why do you think Janie shows this form of behaviour?
> 2 What would you do if you were working with Janie?

Humiliation

Many people would vehemently declare that they would never humiliate a child; nevertheless, they do so unwittingly. To humiliate another individual causes them to feel shame, disgrace, mortification and embarrassment. Many things can embarrass children, such as wetting themselves in front of others or being teased by other children. Handled sensitively, the first situation need not cause embarrassment or humiliation, but a thoughtless remark such as, *'Oh no, not again'* can emotionally hurt a child.

Some early years settings have a 'naughty chair' where children who behave in inappropriate ways are placed for either 'time-out' or as a form of punishment. Whilst 'time-out' or giving a child a breathing space and the opportunity to calm down is an effective strategy with some children, it does not have to be a negative experience. However, the use of a 'naughty chair' singles out a child, draws attention to their behaviour and more often than not is regarded as a shameful place to be, if not by the child then by the staff. This is a form of humiliation.

In many ways humiliation is as harmful as smacking. A child who is humiliated by an adult learns that it is acceptable for bigger people to hurt, or cause distress to, smaller ones. Humiliation causes confusion, as the child may not understand why the adult has responded in that way. Humiliation is a form of abuse.

Withdrawal

Many adults find that one effective way of calming a child who is showing inappropriate behaviour is to withdraw them from the situation; we may call this the time-out strategy. It gives both the adult and the child an opportunity to calm down. However, it is very different from physically removing a child completely. Many schools use withdrawal or, in extreme cases, expulsion as an ultimate sanction against children who are repeatedly difficult to manage. However, it is not fully understood whether it is the withdrawal or expulsion – or the threat of it – that is effective. Does the behaviour change because of the possible expulsion, or does it change for some other reason, such as fear of their parents' reactions?

Putting children in isolation is a very different situation compared to being removed or withdrawn from an activity. Young children need other people, they need to be free from fear, and they need to feel secure. Shutting a child away on their own does not solve the problem of why the child behaved in such a way; it may benefit the adult in that the noisy or disruptive child is removed from their vicinity, but it is of little, if any, benefit to the child. It may increase their emotional stress and decrease their self-confidence and self-esteem. Above all, children should not be left unsupervised, and putting a child on their own is a dereliction of duty of care of childcare and early years workers. It is a form of neglect and neglect is abuse.

> Smacking, humiliation and forms of withdrawal can all be considered forms of abuse. These strategies should have no place in childcare and educational settings and early years professionals should use positive methods to manage children's behaviour.

Using drugs to manage children's behaviour

It is now possible in extreme cases to use prescribed drugs to help control some aspects of children's behaviour. The two most common prescribed drugs are Ritalin and Dexedrine, which can be prescribed under strict conditions of supervision to children diagnosed with attention deficit hyperactivity disorder (ADHD) by their doctor. It is usual practice for the doctor to examine the child and sometimes ask for reports from school and adults working with the child. Adults working with children may have to keep these drugs during the day and make sure that the child takes them at the prescribed time. These adults do not administer the drug.

Ritalin is a psychiatric drug that was developed to have an effect on the central nervous system. Recent studies on this drug claim that there are many adverse side effects. It is suggested that Ritalin might become addictive; it might retard children's growth, increase blood pressure and suppress appetite. In addition, studies suggest that Ritalin might adversely affect cognitive ability. There are at present no studies on the long-term effects on children who are prescribed Ritalin, although it is a matter of concern that the manufacturers and the Medical Control Agency do not recommend the use of this drug in individuals under the age of eighteen. There are some professionals who do not consider ADHD to be a disease – that is, a syndrome – that can be 'cured' by drugs but rather a behavioural problem that can be managed by therapy and/or appropriate strategies.

CHECKPOINT

1 Which theory shows that children can learn by being rewarded?

2 Why do children need to be involved with setting boundaries?

3 Suggest two ways to empower pre-school children.

4 What are amber behaviours?

5 If you say to a child that you don't love them because they have behaved in an inappropriate way, what message could you be giving to the child?

6 Why should rules be simple? Give an example of a simple rule that you and children could use.

7 Maslow suggests that children need to feel secure. How does being consistent help to meet this need?

8 Under what circumstances might a child show negative feelings?

9 In which theory does play therapy have its origins?

10 How can playing instruments help develop social skills?

Chapter 8

Behaviour modification and Individual Education Plans

Introduction

Behaviour modification is becoming one of the most widely-used strategies to help children manage their own behaviour. It is based on the theory of operant conditioning as discussed in Part 1. Behaviour modification can be used by parents, early years practitioners, teachers and other professionals, sometimes following individually designed programmes developed by educational psychologists. There are many behaviour modification programmes that can be developed to meet a child's individual needs, but broadly speaking they all follow a similar pattern or structure. This pattern is frequently referred to as the ABC approach. This means that people engaged in behaviour modification programmes have to give consideration to the antecedents of the behaviour, the actual behaviour and the consequences of the behaviour in respect of the child concerned and other individuals.

This chapter will look at:

◆ the structure of behaviour modification programmes
◆ the use of individual education plans to support the programmes.

The structure of behaviour modification programmes

As mentioned most behaviour modification programmes can be divided into three parts:

1 Antecedents

2 Behaviours

3 Consequences.

The antecedents of the behaviour must be considered before appropriate strategies are considered. In some cases it is the consequences of some behaviours that indicate to us that there is cause for concern. For example, the consequences of the actions of a child who has destructive tendencies could be the first thing that you are aware of, rather than the reasons for the destructive behaviour.

Antecedents

Antecedents of behaviour include:

- family factors, for example, family values and attitudes, cultural/ethnic background, family stress
- school/nursery/early years setting factors, for example, the ethos of the establishment and its rules, the previous response to this behaviour
- child factors, for example, the child's personality, general health and social skills
- situational factors, for example, children have been arguing, there are insufficient resources or toys for all of the children involved.

Antecedents of behaviour can be identified through careful observation and assessment, and through talking with the child in question and their parents/carers. As a way of establishing some of the antecedents, many people use the event sampling observation technique to establish how frequently the behaviour occurs and to provide a comparison during the actual behaviour modification programme. This technique also allows the adult to record the actual behaviour. An example of part of an event sample is given below. In this case the 6-year old child, recorded as A, is very noisy and shouts at other children and adults, causing a significant amount of disruption.

Event	Date and time	Children and adults involved	What happened
1	17.09.02 8:45 am	A, mother, childcare worker (B), 2 other children	A rushed into nursery, shouting goodbye to his mother, hello to B and then went over to the sand tray and began to shout at 2 other children that he wanted to have the wheel.
2	17.09.02 8:50	A	Ran around the room shouting, 'I'm flying, everyone look at me.'
3	17.09.02 9:00	A, all of the children and staff	Register time, all children are on carpet, A sits down with others, when his name is called he shouts his response in a very loud way and then starts to laugh very loudly. Other children near him also start to laugh.
4	17.09.02 10:00	A, 4 other children in the toilets	A is jumping around the toilets and making loud noises. He starts to flick water about and laughs very loudly as he does it.

Part of an event sample

Antecedents of behaviour may be all of the factors or only one of them. It is important that before deciding on any strategy, you are aware of the antecedents and that you have listened to the child in question and acknowledged their feelings.

CASE STUDY

Daisy has been in hospital for several weeks and has been seriously ill. When she returns to the after-school club she finds it difficult to share and is often involved in arguments with other children. The play worker realises that Daisy is unhappy and tries to talk to her about how she feels. It turns out that Daisy feels left out; she thinks that her friends have forgotten her and made new friends excluding her. Daisy wants to be friends with the others but is finding it difficult to talk to them. The play worker is also aware that when in hospital, Daisy had a lot of individual attention from her parents and hospital staff. The play worker thinks that Daisy could also be missing the attention.

1 What do you think could be the antecedent for Daisy's behaviour?

2 How would you find out what the antecedents were?

3 What would you do first?

Behaviour

The description of a child's actual **behaviour** should be:

◆ factual, not emotional, for example, 'He hits Amir when they play a game together', not 'It drives me mad when he starts a fight with Amir'.

◆ precise about the frequency, not vague, for example, 'He has done this four times this week', not, 'It happens a lot'. This is where an event sample observation can be extremely useful.

◆ specific, not general, for example, 'He shouted out his name during registration', not 'He was silly today'. Again an event sample observation will help to record specific behaviour.

◆ situational, not general, for example, 'It happened during registration', not 'He did it this morning'.

ACTIVITY

Below is an extract from a classroom assistant's diary, kept to record the behaviour of one of the children (C) in the class. Read what she has written and then try to rewrite it following the guidelines given above.

> Tuesday.
>
> C has been a problem all day. C was told off loads of times by the teacher, the dinner ladies and by me, but it didn't make any difference. C just ignores everything that we say, and does her own thing. She drives us mad.

Consequences

Consequences include the effect of a child's behaviour on:

◆ the child themselves, such as satisfaction, attention, guilt

◆ other children, for example, fear, pleasure, being controlled

◆ staff and other adults, for example, frustration, anger, gaining their attention

◆ the child's parents, for example, it upsets them, it is an embarrassment, it gains their attention.

SNAPSHOT

Ben has learnt that when he embarrasses his mother she takes more notice of him. He feels that his mother spends more time with his sister and he feels resentful of his sister. On a recent visit to a local fast-food outlet, he started throwing French fries at other people sitting in the eating area. His mother was very embarrassed by this behaviour and, in asking him several times to stop, gave him the attention he wanted.

Once the antecedents, the behaviour and the consequences have been clearly identified, a behaviour modification programme can be developed. The programme can be developed by following a ten-point action plan, such as the one described below. Following this plan gives structure and rigour to the programme and means that parents, early years practitioners, play workers and other professionals can all follow it.

A ten-point action plan

An example of a plan for a behaviour modification programme:

1 Precisely and accurately describe the inappropriate or unwanted behaviour, in other words, the behaviour that you want to change.

2 Consider the antecedents that may be important factors in causing the behaviour.

3 Consider carefully the situation in which the behaviour occurs. For example, is the environment suitable, is there enough to stimulate the child etc. This will help to identify any relevant and significant features.

4 List all the consequences that may be positive from the child's point of view.

5 Set understandable and obvious targets for change, and aim to achieve these targets in small, manageable steps.

6 Decide who will be responsible for implementing and monitoring the change. It is possible, and indeed important for consistency, to involve other people, but one person does need to take overall responsibility for the programme.

7 Talk to and tell the child about the targets. Explain why you are aiming to change the behaviour. Involve the child.

8 Pick a time to start the programme and decide upon a time to evaluate it, if the strategy is having an impact.

9 Implement the behaviour modification programme consistently during this time.

10 After the implementation stage, review its success, and adapt as needed.

For any behaviour modification programme to work effectively, it must meet the following criteria:

◆ Rules or boundaries must be established and the child must be aware of them.

◆ The child must be aware of the outcomes attached to the behaviours, regardless of whether they are positive or negative, for example, 'If you do this, this will happen'. This is where the operant conditioning theory can be applied as you give positive rewards/reinforcers or negative reinforcers such as sanctions or punishments.

◆ The outcomes must be appropriate to the age and developmental stage of the child.

- The outcomes must be applied consistently, every time the behaviour occurs.
- The outcomes must be applied immediately.
- Outcomes must take into account individual likes and dislikes, for example, what an adult sees as a negative outcome, in others words a dislike, the child may see as positive.
- The programme must involve all adults who have close contact with the child. This means consistent, frequent dialogue and discussion between the setting and the home.

An example of a behaviour modification programme following a ten-point action plan

The scenario

At the beginning of term, twelve new children start school, all aged four years. One of the children, Ami, is an only child who has very caring, but rather over-protective parents who want her to do well. Ami is not used to coping with the rough and tumble of large groups of children. She is becoming increasingly upset and angry at having to share and wait her turn. She insists on being at the head of the line for when the class go out to play, lunchtime or assembly, and pushes the other children out of the way.

1 **Precisely and accurately describe the behaviour**

   Ami is angry, she is upset; she pushes other children out of the way.

2 **Consider the antecedents**
   - Ami has not had many opportunities to play with other children, as her parents have been over-protective, and she is an only child.
   - Her parents have high expectations of her to do well and be 'first' in class, and this could be putting pressure on her.

3 **Consider the situation when the behaviour occurs**
   - The behaviour of pushing other children occurs at play, lunchtime and assembly.
   - The behaviour of not sharing happens during group activities.
   - The behaviour of not waiting her turn happens when she wants attention from the adult.

4 **List all of the consequences**
   - Ami gets the attention of the adults in the room when she gets angry and when she pushes other children.
   - Ami gets reactions and attention from the other children.

- Ami gets a reaction and more attention from her parents because her behaviour embarrasses them.
- This behaviour may make Ami feel important and so help meet her need to meet the expectations of her parents.

5 **Set understandable and obvious targets for change**

The class teacher and the classroom assistant will help Ami to:

- share
- take turns
- understand that other children do not like her to push them
- understand that it is not fair for her to be always first in line.

6 **Decide who will be responsible for implementing and monitoring the change**

- The class teacher will speak to Ami's parents.
- The class teacher and the classroom assistant will talk to Ami and they will decide on the first target for change.
- The classroom assistant will implement and monitor the change.

7 **Talk to and tell the child about the targets**

The class teacher and the classroom assistant will talk with Ami about:

- how she is feeling, her likes, dislikes and concerns
- the 'rules' about behaviour in the classroom and why they are there
- why Ami's behaviour is causing concern and why they want to help her to manage her behaviour without hurting or upsetting Ami, other children, her parents or the teacher and assistant
- the consequences of her behaviour, its outcomes and what might happen if she continues to behave in this way. For example, if she keeps pushing the other children, one of them might fall over and hurt themselves, or she could fall and hurt herself as she pushes them out of the way
- one small achievable target they can decide to work on, such as Ami learning how to control her temper.

  To achieve the target, Ami could be given time-out in order for her to calm down. The classroom assistant could talk quietly and calmly to her to help her deal with and control her feelings. When calm she could return to the activity.

8 **Pick a time to start the programme**

- Ami and the classroom assistant could decide to start the programme at the beginning of the week, or the next day, or immediately.
- They could decide to talk about how things are going with Ami's teacher at the end of the week, or after three or four days.

9 **Implement the behaviour modification programme consistently**

   ◆ The classroom assistant will have responsibility for making sure that the programme is applied consistently. The teacher will support both Ami and the classroom assistant.

10 **After the implementation stage, review the programme's success**

   ◆ Ami, the teacher and the classroom assistant will talk again after the agreed length of time, and may decide that Ami is not getting as angry.

   ◆ They may agree to carry on for another week.

What actually happened

It was decided that Ami should learn ways to control her angry feelings as this was leading to other difficulties within the class. The adults believed that Ami became angry when she felt that she was not being good enough. This view was discussed with both Ami and her parents. It was decided that when Ami became angry the classroom assistant would take Ami to the book corner and they would sit quietly together. (Strategy – time-out, target to control angry feelings.) They would talk about how Ami felt and give her a chance to calm down. When Ami was calm she would return to the activity she had been involved in. Her parents agreed that they would try this strategy at home and they said that Ami often became angry at home. It was agreed by everyone that time-out would start the following day. The classroom assistant made sure that a record was kept by noting the dates and times when Ami became angry. After a week the number of times that Ami had become angry had decreased. It had been decided that this would be the criterion for deciding whether the strategy had been effective. Everybody talked again and they agreed to carry on for another week. During the time that this target was being worked on, Ami was rewarded by praise when she did control her feelings, by her parents, the teacher and the classroom assistant. It actually took three-and-a-half weeks for Ami to manage her feelings, but as she learnt how to do this she also began to stop pushing other children.

THINK IT OVER:

The case study about Ami was used at a recent workshop on behaviour, and caused much discussion and debate. One of the participants felt that using the strategy of giving Ami time-out with the classroom assistant was in fact a reward as Ami got more attention than other children in the class, despite the fact that she was not behaving in an appropriate way. The view was expressed that maybe the 'marble in the jar' idea (as described in Chapter 7), or something similar, would have been more appropriate, as it would have shown Ami the consequences of her actions on the other children and would have helped her become more aware of the feelings of others. The other viewpoint that was expressed was that Ami was too young to understand the consequences of her actions on others and so time-out was an appropriate strategy to use.

What do you think?

ACTIVITY

Below are two scenarios; choose the one that is closest to your work situation and then answer the following questions:

1 Describe the child's behaviour in terms of the ABC model.

2 What, in your view, would be the most appropriate strategy to use to manage this behaviour?

3 Draw up an action plan to target any changes that you feel might be appropriate.

4 What criteria would you use to decide whether your action plan has been successful?

Scenario 1

At a week-long holiday club for up to 24 children aged from five to eleven, one of the nine-year-olds questions everything that is suggested. This behaviour could be described as argumentative and is sometimes aggressive. Younger children have started to copy the child. The play workers find this behaviour frustrating and difficult to deal with.

Scenario 2

In a day nursery one of the two-year-olds has started biting other children and staff. Other parents have started to complain about the obvious bite marks on their children. The nursery staff find this behaviour unacceptable and want to stop the child from biting.

The use of Individual Education Plans to support behaviour modification programmes

Many people find that it is helpful to produce an Individual Education Plan (IEP) when working through the ten-point action plan described earlier. IEPs are provided for children who have been identified as having special educational needs. However, there is no reason why practitioners should not devise IEPs for any child who is causing concern for whatever reason. IEP's should only be used once a setting has already made adjustments to their own practice. IEPs are invaluable for several reasons:

◆ An IEP sets achievable targets for a child and is therefore a positive tool to empower them.

◆ An IEP focuses on the strengths of a child, rather than what they cannot do, and is yet another way to empower them.

- The targets set in an IEP are reviewed regularly, which means that the progress a child makes will also be carefully monitored.
- An IEP is a positive way of working in partnership with parents.

There is no standard format for an IEP. Some local education authorities do have standard forms that are used for all children who have been identified with special educational needs, but each setting is free to devise their own. The examples of IEPs shown in this chapter are exactly that, examples. It is a good idea for you to look at other examples of IEPs from other settings before you devise your own. It is important that the IEP is a useful and workable tool for both you and the child that you are planning to help. It should not be another piece of paper in a file. Whatever format you decide upon, certain information is essential:

- the child's name and date of birth
- a brief summary of the child's needs and/or areas for development
- the targets
- who will be involved
- progress made, or criteria to measure success of the target
- date of review
- signatures of staff and parent.

A step-by-step approach to writing an IEP

Information-gathering

1. **Identify the behaviour or issues that are causing concern**. It is very important that this step is completely factual, non-judgemental and is a realistic identification of the behaviour. It will not be of any use to either the child you are planning to help or those with whom they are involved if statements such as:

    'Jessie whinges all day and it really annoys other staff,' or

    'parents are always complaining about Jessie's behaviour in the playground'

    are written.

    These statements should be written along the following lines:

    'Jessie uses a whining voice to attract the attention of staff' and

    'Jessie hits other children when they will not let her play with them. This happens in the playground at midmorning and lunchtimes'

    It is a good idea to write this information down and many people find that some form of observation is a reliable format to use; for example, you could do an event sample to determine exactly when each incident for concern occurs. An event sample may also give information about the antecedent to the behaviour and sometimes the consequences. A written observation or diary may also be a useful way to identify the behaviour.

This step should be seen as part of the information-gathering process.

2 **Talk to other people who are involved with the child.** Before any realistic targets can be set it is important to build up as wide a picture as possible of the child in question. Talk to the child's parents/carers first, then talk to other professionals who are involved with the child and if appropriate, siblings. Other professionals could be other teachers, support staff, early years workers, in fact everyone who is involved with the child. Again the information that is collected should be factual and non-judgemental. The aim of any IEP is to allow the child to succeed and progress, and information that is gathered should reflect this positive view. Discussions with parents could focus on activities and experiences that the child enjoys, their positive attributes and things that they do well. It is all too easy to spend time talking to parents about what their child doesn't do rather than what they can do. This is counterproductive, as it can be very demoralising and distressing for parents. If the aim is to work in partnership with parents, then the information that is shared should be positive and so allow for realistic targets to be drawn up. Parents should be involved in setting targets and in deciding how to implement them. This may mean that more than one meeting will need to be arranged between staff and parents.

3 **Talk to the child.** Although this may seem obvious, it is surprising how may adults actually fail to talk to the child they want to help. Discussions should focus on the child's strengths and weaknesses, their likes and dislikes, and how they can be empowered through an IEP.

4 Decide what **additional resources** may be needed to support this child, including other people as well as activities and/or equipment. Don't forget that time should be considered as a resource. There is little chance of an IEP being successful if it does not consider the time implications both for the adult and the child. This doesn't just mean the length of time that the plan will run for, or the length of time before the review, but takes into consideration the demands of a busy classroom, or nursery environment.

5 Decide **exactly who** will be involved with the setting of the targets, the implementation of the plan, the monitoring and review, and making sure that the child's parents are involved in the target-setting and that they get a copy of the plan. In order to maintain a consistent and focused approach it is good practice to have one person responsible for the implementation of the targets. Some settings prefer to have another individual reviewing the targets to give a more objective view, but sometimes this is not possible, especially in small settings. Whoever reviews the targets should focus on what the child has achieved rather than what they have not.

Writing realistic targets

Writing realistic targets is essential to the success of any individual education plan.

1 It is very important that the IEP **does not attempt to change or modify all aspects of the child's behaviour at once.** If this is the case the IEP will not work. It is much more effective to set one or maybe two achievable targets that can be given 100 per cent concentration and effort for a short space of time. Looking at the earlier example of Jessie, we know that she whinges and also that she hits other children and this causes concern. A target for Jessie might be to focus on modifying her behaviour in the playground. This in itself is not a positive target. The issue for other children is that Jessie hits them; the issue for the parents is that they do not like their children being hit by another child; and the issue for Jessie is that she doesn't have anyone to play with. All of these issues are negative and do not empower Jessie in any way.

2 **Targets need to be written that are positive** and allow the child to succeed. A target should state what the child **will do** rather than what they **will not do.** In this situation, setting a target for Jessie to play co-operatively in the playground, regardless of the time of day, is unrealistic, as it is more than likely that Jessie does not know how to play co-operatively. In addition, lunch time in a playground is a long time for a child. A suggested target could focus on the mid-morning break, which is a much shorter length of time. In order for Jessie to stop hitting children when they will not let her join in she needs to learn how to play co-operatively. There are many ways that Jessie could be helped to play co-operatively and they do not necessarily need to be in the playground. If Jessie's parents have said that she enjoys playing board games with her grandparents, a suggested achievable first target for Jessie could be:

   'Jessie will play a board game which involves sharing and turn-taking with three other children and a classroom assistant. Each time Jessie shares and /or turn-takes, in any way at all, she will be rewarded with praise, smiles and positive body language from the classroom assistant.'

3 **Targets should build on success.** In Jessie's case, when the first target is achieved and Jessie shares and takes her turn, in other words plays co-operatively, a second target could be:

   'Jessie will play a co-operative game with a small group of children in the playground at mid-morning break, with the support of a classroom assistant. All positive aspects of Jessie's play will be rewarded, while non-co-operative behaviour will be ignored.'

4 There is no way that a child's behaviour will change overnight, or even, realistically, in a week or two. In order for a target to be achievable it is important that there is a **consistent, focused approach** for the length of time that the target will run. An inconsistent approach such as ignoring some

behaviour but not others will confuse the child and therefore make the achievement of the target very difficult. It also important that this consistent approach is followed by all adults that the child comes into contact with including parents and, if possible, other family members.

5 **The length of the plan and the date of the review should be agreed** before it is started. Agreement is needed from all adults involved and the child. The length of time should be realistic for the plan to motivate the child and meet their needs. The review date should be far away enough to allow the target to be implemented; the child to adjust to the demands of the target, such as turn-taking or sharing; and progress to be made. In most cases, three weeks is often regarded as a reasonable length of time for a review of a target that is implemented every weekday. On the other hand, if the child attends the setting perhaps twice a week, a longer period may be necessary; or if the target is obviously achieved within a shortened time span, then the review date can be brought forward. The key to setting a review date is a flexible approach that will meet the needs of the child. Regular reviewing of the targets is essential. This is a fundamental part of the whole process of helping a child to succeed and be empowered.

Most children respond well to the targets of their IEP, provided that the aim of the plan has been to empower the child, and not to make life easier for the adult, and that the strategies deployed by the adults to implement the plan take into consideration individual needs. Strategies used to reward a child should be those which positively reinforce actions and behaviour. As discussed in Part 1, positive reinforcement (following Skinner's theory) is something that increases the likelihood of a modified behaviour or an action being repeated because the outcome is pleasant and satisfies a need.

You might find it helpful when setting targets to remember the acronym **SMART**.

S   specific
The target should ideally break down the planned changes into specific and achievable steps. For example, suppose that you have agreed a target to help a child develop concentration skills. Your target should be broken down into specific steps, such as to help the child to concentrate for five minutes, or perhaps even less. When this has been achieved, increase the length of time and so on. The specific target could be recorded initially as to help child X concentrate for three minutes during story time. This is very specific and leaves no one in any doubt what you are hoping to achieve.

M   measurable
If a target is not measurable or quantifiable, how can we tell if a child has made any progress? In the same way, what criteria might we use to assess

whether the target has been met and progress made? In the example above, you might record that the child was able to concentrate at story time for only two minutes, rather than the target of three. The fact that your target had a time limit automatically made it possible to measure that the target was not achievable for that child, and had not been broken down into small enough steps.

A   achievable
The main focus of any target, outcome or educational plan should be to empower the child and help them to manage their own behaviour. It therefore follows that the targets should be realistically achievable for the child; they should be confident that they can reach the targets. We want to build up self-confidence and self-esteem and for the child to achieve and make progress; we do not want to set them up to fail.

R   relevant
Ask yourself: are the targets that you are working towards relevant to the child? Do they really understand **why** you want to help them attain or develop these skills? The child needs to know and understand that the target will be of benefit to them. The child might be thinking, 'Why do I need to concentrate at story time? I am quite happy talking to my mate – I find story time boring, and the story does not interest me, so I don't want to listen.'

T   time-bound
Setting a date for the review of an IEP gives everyone concerned a focus and goal to work towards. The date, however, should not be too far in the future, as the momentum could be lost; on the other hand there has to be sufficient time for the target to have an effect. There is no hard and fast rule as to how much time should be allowed before a review; it depends on the child, their needs and the target. It might be that you quickly realise that the target set is not achievable and you might review your plan after only a few days.

The four IEPs on the following pages have been devised by a local education authority for use in all of their schools, from nursery to secondary. These forms can be used by all staff and parents/carers and are suitable for use if the child has been identified as having special educational needs. They are included to show you possible ways of developing and writing an IEP for a range of ages and a variety of identified areas to be developed.

CT stands for class teacher.

TA stands for teaching assistant.

148

INDIVIDUAL EDUCATION PLAN (IEP)

Nursery/Pre-school:				
Name:	**Date of birth**	**Age:** 3.2	**Staff involved:**	**SENCO:**
IEP start date:	**Review date:**		**Signed:**	**Signed:**

Strengths:
Relates well to adults. Enjoys role-play. Expressive language – likes to talk about father in the army.

Areas to be developed (*each area should have a corresponding target*):
Positive social interaction with peers.

Targets	Strategies	Provision	Success criteria	Achieved
1. To sit for 2 minutes at story time.	· Space to sit. · Toy to hold. · Own copy of small book with supporter.	· Small version of big book used. · Practitioner to sit near during story time.	· To sit for 2 minutes 4/5 times.	
2. To line up without pushing in at home time. Some nurseries feel it is inappropriate to 'line-up' at this age. Remember to always follow your settings policies when writing up an IEP.	· Remind of rule prior to time. · Ensure time in queue is short. · Praise all 'good soldiers'.	· Practitioner to monitor and give immediate praise. · Allow 'good soldiers' to go first.	· To line up appropriately 4/5 times.	
3. To separate from parent without a tantrum, with support.	· Allow to bring in comfort toy.	· Name card. · Photographs. · Visual task board. · Consistent key worker.	· To join group with parent 3/5 times. · To join group with key worker 2/5 times.	

Parent/Carer involvement:	Child's view:	Additional information:
To encourage social activities, playing with other children.	Enjoys attending nursery. Wants to be a 'good soldier'.	Only child. Father often away from home.

Evaluation and future action:

INDIVIDUAL EDUCATION PLAN (IEP)

School (primary):		
Name:	Date of birth	Yr group: 1	Class teacher:	SENCO:

| IEP start date: | Review date: | Signed: | Signed: |

Strengths:
Can dress herself after PE. Will come and sit down on carpet with class. Looks at big book and listens to a story. Has a small sight vocabulary including her name.

Areas to be developed (*each area should have a corresponding target*):
Following instructions. Working independently within a group. Responding to adults. Personal hygiene.

Targets	Strategies	Provision	Success criteria	Achieved
1. To follow basic instructions in PE.	• Sit near CT in hall and listen carefully. • Tell the TA what she has to do. • Teacher calls her name before instructions are given. • Prompt her to look at the other children. • Praise and reward for each time she achieves target until secure.	• TA to support listening/talk through what she has to do. • TA to encourage looking/following actions of other children (visual). • CT rewards/praises.	• Carries out correct activity 3 times per lesson.	
2. To be able to work for 5 minutes at a table, with a group of children, independently.	• The task should be one she enjoys and feels confident with. • She is sitting by a 'friend'. • TA sits with her until she is confident then withdraws for 2 mins (3 mins, 4 mins, 5 mins) (done over a period of time).	• Careful choice of task. • Table to be situated in area of few distractions. • Pupil to choose a 'friend'. • Use of sand timers. • TA support.	• To work for 5 minutes (each day) without assistance.	
3. To answer her name at registration.	• To give non-verbal response to her name when called. • To hold up a card with her name on when CT calls it. • To answer 'Yes' when her name is called. • To answer 'Yes, Mrs ...'.	• Name card. • Support from TA. • Give her time to respond.	• To answer 'Yes, Mrs ...' when her name is called at registration times.	
4. To wash her hands after using the toilet.	• Picture sequence of washing and drying hands (talk through). • 'Social stories' technique. • Use of bowl and water first. • Using taps/soap/paper towel. • Reward for carrying it out/remembering.	• Photos of her going through the process of washing/drying hands. • Short 'story book'. • TA support. • Taps that turn easily. • Paper towels. • Stickers/charts etc.	• To wash hands and dry them without TA's support, following each toilet visit.	

Parent/Carer involvement:	Pupil's view:
To encourage her to answer 'Yes Mum' when called.	To answer 'Yes Mum' when called.

Additional information:
High anxiety. Fear of hand dryer noise.

Evaluation and future action:

Chapter 8 Behaviour modification and Individual Education Plans

INDIVIDUAL EDUCATION PLAN (IEP)

3

School (primary):			
Name:	**Date of birth**	**Class teacher:**	**SENCO:**
IEP start date:	**Review date:**	**Signed:**	**Signed:**

Strengths:
Enjoys reading and science. Very good at ICT.

Yr group: 6

Areas to be developed (*each area should have a corresponding target*):
Completion of work. Taking part in class discussion (appropriately). Develop appropriate conversation skills. Finds difficulty working in a group.

Targets	Strategies	Provision	Success criteria	Achieved
1. To complete a given task without complaint in a given time.	• Choice of task (non-stressful initially). • Time set for completion, e.g. 15 mins. • All materials and equipment at hand. • Remain at table until finished. • TA support available. • Use of ICT when appropriate/reward.	• Personal timetable. • Sand timers/small clock. • Quiet work area. • Choice of task. • TA/CT support if requested. • Computer/printer.	• To finish a task in the time set 2 or more occasions during the day.	
2. To put up hand and answer questions during class discussion.	• Listen carefully to CT questions. • Check with TA whether answer is appropriate. • Put up hand and wait for CT to ask. • Answer question in appropriate voice. • Keep check on how many 'tries' each day.	• TA support (slowly withdrawn). • Coloured cards system to encourage answering. • Note book to record number of tries. • Positive feedback from CT.	• To try to answer 2 questions in each session.	
3. To have conversations with others, thinking about their feelings and needs.	• Small social skills group. • Role-play, use of puppets, photographs. • Worksheets to work on conversations. • Listens to tapes of conversations within group.	• CT/TA input. • Pictures of role-play situations/ watching conversations on video. • Tape player.	• Has simple conversations with adults, and other children in school, being aware of their needs.	
4. To be an active member of a . group.	• Care in selecting partners or group members. • Give each one a clear role. • Help given with sequence needed for successful completion. • Discuss any problems encountered.	• CT/TA support for the group. • Give each other their role on paper. • Give prompt sheet. • Start with one curriculum area, e.g. science.	• To carry out group activities successfully as an active member, once daily.	

Parent/Carer involvement:	Pupil's view:
Parents to encourage him to invite friends round, and to take part in simple family discussions.	'I understand my targets and would like to use my computer as my reward.'

Additional information:
Likes to work to his own agenda.

Evaluation and future action:

School (secondary):						4

INDIVIDUAL EDUCATION PLAN (IEP)

Name:　　　　**Date of birth**　　　　**Yr group:** 9　　**Form:** 9T

IEP start date:　　　**Review date:**　　　**KS2/3 SATs**　English: 4　　English: 4　　Maths: 4　　Science: 4

Strengths:
Is capable of good achievement in all subjects.

Areas to be developed (*each area should have a corresponding target*):
Time-keeping, handing in homework, reduction in use of bad language.

Targets	Strategies	Provision	Success criteria	Achieved
1. To arrive in the classroom promptly at the start of a lesson.	• Staff to encourage prompt arrival with positive, welcoming remarks. • Prompt arrivals to be celebrated on report sheets. • Points given towards school system.	• Form teacher to monitor report sheet daily at end of school. • Number of prompt arrivals sent home to parents.	• To arrive promptly at every lesson.	
2. One piece of homework to be completed and handed in daily.	• Homework handed in to form teacher at morning registration. This to be celebrated on report sheet. • Points given towards school system.	• Attendance at homework club to be encouraged. • Parents informed daily.	• Form teacher receiving homework every morning.	
3. Instances of swearing out loud during lessons to be reduced.	• X and staff to record number of instances. Both figures to be recorded on report sheet. • Points given towards school system.	• Form teacher to monitor daily at end of school. Parents informed of progress daily on note home.	• 20% reduction over two weeks.	

Parent/Carer involvement:
Encourage homework completion. Ask for daily note home and reward. Following review, dad will take to football match.

Pupil's view:
Willing to try. Agreed homework, 2 × Maths, 2 × English, 1 of own choice weekly.

Additional information:
Responds well to individual attention

Evaluation and future action:

Names of all staff involved:
Form teacher, head of year.

Signed: _____ (SENCO)　　Date: _____

CHECKPOINT

1 Which theory is based on behaviour modification?

2 What do the letters ABC stand for?

3 How can antecedents of behaviour be identified?

4 What is wrong with this description of a child's behaviour? – 'I think he does this on purpose to annoy me.'

5 List four things that could be the consequences of behaviour for the child themselves.

6 Why is it a good idea for an IEP to consider the child's strengths?

7 What does the acronym SMART stand for?

8 Why do targets need to be achievable?

Chapter 9

Teamwork and seeking additional support

Introduction

Many settings and teams are able to empower children to manage their own behaviour without support from other professionals. However, there are times when additional support and help may be needed. There are a wide range of professionals who can provide children, their parents and early years settings, with additional support. The Children Act (1989) clearly states that all professionals in health, social services and education should work collectively to meet children's needs, whatever those needs may be. This is often referred to as a multi-disciplinary approach. It is important that when we do work with other professionals that we work as a team, providing a consistent approach to helping and guiding children. An important aspect of working with other professionals and parents and carers is our ability to communicate effectively. This will be discussed in Chapter 10.

This chapter will consider:
- the general principles of teamwork
- behaviour policies
- SENCOs and inclusion
- working with outside agencies and other professionals.

These points will then be applied to a range of settings and workplace environments.

The general principles of teamwork

Before we consider the principles of working in a team, let us look at what we mean by a 'team'. People often recognise that they should be, or are, in a team, but aren't quite sure what it is.

Below is a list of terms that are often used when describing 'a team':

◆ a group of people

◆ synergy

◆ having one aim

◆ whole/sum

◆ co-operation

◆ flexibility

◆ working together

◆ reporting to one boss.

Which ones do you think define what a team is?

Some of these terms are features of *good* teams, for example, 'whole/sum' is a feature of a team that is working well together. On the other hand, 'reporting to one boss' can be misleading. In well-designed organisations, people reporting to one boss often do form teams, such as teachers reporting to a year head forming a year team. But reporting lines are frequently complicated and people can be members of several teams, with effectively several bosses. For example, a classroom assistant may be working in a team with the teacher and so have the head teacher or year leader as the 'boss', but at the same time could be working in a team of classroom-assistant-supporting children, and reporting to the Special Educational Needs Co-ordinator (SENCO). People can be members of several teams, because a team can be defined as 'a group of people who are working together towards a common goal'. This definition is applicable whether we are talking about a group of individuals in a nursery, in a school or even in a football team. Each individual should believe that his or her contribution is essential to the team and is compatible with the overall philosophy. For example, to play a successful game of football, all of the players must work together to score goals or prevent the other team from scoring; one member of the team cannot go and do 'their own thing' on the pitch, or the success of the entire team is compromised. This is also true in childcare and educational settings.

An effective team depends on the co-operation and skills of all of its members. We cannot expect to provide children with a consistent approach to guiding and helping them, if we are not working as a team. Even practitioners who may be working on their own, such as private nannies and childminders, should be aware of the principles of teamwork. The other team members will not necessarily be people who work alongside them, as is the case with classroom assistants and teachers, but are people who are directly involved with the children, for example, parents, the wider family and other professionals with whom the child is involved.

The following are attributes of effective teams:

- **Team goals** that are developed through a group process of interaction and agreement, in which each team member is willing to work towards achieving these goals. For example, when a key worker has developed an individual education plan (IEP) for a child, with specific targets, in order for the targets to be effective, **all** of the team involved with the child must work towards achieving them.

- **Participation** is actively shown by all of the team members, and roles are shared to make possible the completion of tasks and feelings of group togetherness. For example, a successful and effective team in a pre-school group would have an agreed rota for washing the paint pots or cleaning the toilets. It should not be the same person who always has the less attractive jobs.

- **Team decision-making** that encourages active participation by all members. This means that it is important that all team members attend team meetings. This provides opportunities for constructive feedback that will help the team and help problem-solving, through discussing issues. For example, a team meeting is the appropriate forum for discussing issues relating to behaviour, not a coffee-break shared by two or three team members only.

- **Team member resources** (talents, skills, knowledge and experiences) are fully identified, recognised, and used whenever appropriate. For example, a newly qualified member of staff may have lots of fresh new ideas, compared to staff who have been in the setting for several years. The new member of the team has a lot to offer the team, as do the other team members, who may be able to share their experience of caring for children with inappropriate behaviours.

As team members work together to build trust and support, they should be able to develop and accomplish desired results and/or goals. However, it is vital that all team members fully understand what the desired results and goals are. This is where policies are essential. Some of a setting's policies are based on legal requirements, such as Equal Opportunities, Child Protection and Health and Safety; others are based on good practice, such as a setting's policies on admissions, staff discipline and grievances.

Behaviour policies

A behaviour policy ensures that all team members clearly understand how they will promote positive behaviour and empower children. Any policy should be reviewed regularly to make sure that all team members, including children and parents, understand its content.

A policy should contain:

- *A statement of aims.* This could be a simple statement such as: 'All adults working in the group will promote acceptable behaviour at all times and show respect for others'.
- *What the setting expects of the children and the staff.* For example:

  'We expect all children and adults to follow the rules of the setting. These are:

  - Nobody will do anything that is hurtful, offensive or dangerous to another person
  - Nobody will damage another person's things
  - We will all care for each other.'

- *What methods will be used to manage children's behaviour.* This could include a clear statement that physical punishment will not be used. The methods to be used could be listed, such as distraction, explanation, praise, rewards, supervised time-out, together with a statement that the method used will be chosen as the most appropriate to meet the child's needs and will be applied consistently.
- *Which behaviours are not acceptable.* For example, bullying, violent acts, and swearing.
- *How parents and carers will be informed and consulted.* Groups should keep an incident book to record incidences of unwanted or inappropriate behaviour, which parents can read and sign.
- *Any training that staff can access.* Many settings are members of the Pre-School Learning Alliance and can access training through them. All settings have training opportunities provided through the local Early Years Development and Childcare Partnerships.

It is therefore important that consideration is given as to who is going to draw up the policy or statement and how other staff members and children will be consulted on its contents. It is generally accepted that if people are drawn into the creation of any policy, they will have a greater understanding of its contents and are more likely to put it into practice successfully. The whole policy, or statement, should be given to each parent or be available for them to read and discuss with staff. The Pre-School Learning Alliance produces exemplar policies that groups can use to develop their own policy or statement.

A good example of a behaviour management policy which fulfils the key points stated above has been drawn up by Chadwell St Mary Primary School. Part of this policy is duplicated below, which is a table of sanctions intended to be displayed in every classroom. Not only does this clearly set out which behaviours are unacceptable, it also explains how the children behaving unacceptably will be managed, and how parents and staff will be involved.

Behaviour checks	
Stage	Sanction
1	**WARNING, NAME ON CARD** All classes will have a card index box with a card for each child. Behaviour checks will be recorded on the card. This will provide a record of behaviour throughout the year and could be rewarded accordingly.
2	**MOVE PLACE, WORK ALONE** Record as Stage 1 with number of rule broken and a short explanation of antecedents if necessary.
3	**LOSE ALL OR PART OF PLAYTIME** A slip is filled in and sent IMMEDIATELY to the duty teacher (currently Head teacher). At playtime, child is reminded to go to the hall (or taken).
4	**TIME OUT IN ANOTHER CLASS** Child is sent to time-out room (prearranged with another teacher, preferably in a different year group/Keystage). This to be for a session or until work is completed etc.
5	**SENT TO HEADTEACHER, LETTER HOME** The letter will invite parents to come into school to discuss child's behaviour with Head teacher. Child required to attend five Stage 3 playtimes' sanctions and to be closely supervised by an MDA during lunchtime period.
After this stage the behaviour checks will be monitored by senior management with class teacher help. SENCO will become involved in monitoring process (IBP).	
6	**CHILD ON REPORT** Letter to parents stating that the child will be required to report to senior management daily for a fixed period to monitor behaviour. Standard form will be completed with child. Child required to attend five Stage 3 playtimes' sanctions and to be closely supervised by an MDA during lunchtime period.
7	**FORMAL CONTRACT** Parents will be asked to attend a formal meeting at which the child is given a formal contract. Parents are asked to agree to the terms and to monitor behaviour in partnership with the school. (Home-school book). Sanctions as at Stage 5/6 still apply.
8	**FIXED TERM IN ANOTHER YEAR GROUP** Sanctions as at Stage 5/6 still apply.
9	**FIXED TERM EXCLUSION**
10	**PERMANENT EXCLUSION**

SNAPSHOT

Stourminster School, in the south of England, has developed a policy of managing behaviour based on Assertive Discipline. The school population consists of many children with complex emotional, social and behavioural difficulties. Accentuating the positive is a key element of the Assertive Discipline approach and involves helping teachers raise the ratio of positive to negative comments they give to children on a daily basis. Each child carries a green card that is used to record their points earned each lesson depending on their performance regarding the school rules (shown below). The points are added up each week and discussed at an individual meeting with either the head or deputy. The points recorded on the green card generate rewards on a graded scale. Positive rather than negative communication with parents is the norm, with staff telephoning home or sending a postcard to parents to celebrate their child's successes. The school has a very clear policy on how staff will respond to misbehaviour and, as with the positive consequences, there is a system which ensures consistency and fairness. The Assertive Discipline approach dictates that it is not the severity of the sanction that is important, but the consistency with which it is applied. The approach is maintained by the Head Teacher modelling good behaviour management skills, celebrating the success of teachers with difficult children, regular reminders of the approach through staff meetings and giving clear guidance and support to new staff members and supply staff.

School rules

There is an overriding expectation that all children will do their best at all times.

1 Follow instructions.

2 Keep hands, feet and other objects to yourself.

3 Don't say things that might upset people, including teasing and swearing.

4 Don't leave or move away from where you're supposed to be.

5 Walk around the school.

ACTIVITY

Have another look at the behaviour policy in your workplace. Make sure that you fully understand the expectations of the policy and that you are working towards it.

If you are a childminder, you may not have a written policy as such but may have a framework or set of house rules that you discuss with parents at the first meeting. It is still good practice to review these rules regularly and make sure that they are consistently applied.

SENCOs *and inclusion*

As part of the Special Educational Needs Code of Practice 2001, every early years setting and school in receipt of government funding has to have a named person who is responsible for co-ordinating the support for children with special educational needs, which can include behavioural difficulties. This named person is referred to as the Special Educational Needs Co-ordinator or SENCO. A SENCO has several responsibilities, which include supporting other team members, meeting with parents and carers and other professionals, and observing children.

A SENCO does not necessarily develop IEPs but supports other team members who are involved with doing this. Similarly a SENCO is not the only person involved in developing a special educational needs policy or behaviour management policy, but is part of the team that is doing this. Many settings and establishments who are not in receipt of government funding, such as private schools, also have SENCOs who can take on similar responsibilities to those in government-funded settings.

SENCOs may also liaise with other settings, such as after-school clubs, play schemes and childminders, in order to meet the individual needs of children.

SNAPSHOT

Elen is the SENCO in a large day nursery which also has before- and after-school sessions and holiday clubs for children up to the age of eleven years. One eight-year-old, Aisha, has an IEP with targets that relate to behavioural issues. Elen has talked to the SENCO at the local primary school and can now ensure that the targets for Aisha are consistently applied in the before- and after-school sessions as well as during the holiday club. Elen says she feels it is important for Aisha to understand that she has to try to meet her targets wherever she is and that it isn't something that she does only at school. As a result Elen is now invited to attend the review meetings at the school with the child's parents and the school's SENCO. This is a good example of teamwork with professionals from different settings.

Schools and early years settings have inclusive practices where children with special educational needs are educated alongside their peers and therefore have access to all areas of the curriculum. This effectively means that all children are expected to follow the same framework of behaviour and keep to the same rules. It is thought that about 20 per cent of school-age children have a special educational need at some point in their life, whereas about two per cent have a need that is significant. It is this two per cent of children that are assessed by their local authority, which issues a statement setting out how their needs should be met. This process is usually referred to as 'statementing' and is clearly set out in the Special Educational Needs Code of Practice I (January 2001). Children under the age of two very rarely have a statement, but they might be supported by other professionals, such as **portage** workers, if they have a medical condition.

Portage is a home teaching service in which pre-school children are supported in their own homes. Portage workers can work with children with a variety of conditions, such as language delay. Portage workers usually concentrate on specific skills such as developing fine and gross motor skills, self-help and independence.

The Code of Practice for the Identification and Assessment of Children with Special Educational Needs

The revised Code of Practice clearly sets out a 'step-by-step' or 'graduated approach' as to how to set about getting help for children with special educational needs (this can include emotional and behavioural difficulties and problems that are affecting their learning). The graduated approach is basically in three stages:

1 *Early Years Action* (for children under statutory school age) or *School Action*. In many cases an early years worker may be the first person to identify that a child has a problem or difficulty. One occasion for setting Early Years or School Action in motion is when aspects of a child's behaviour are still difficult to manage, even though staff have tried and persisted with positive strategies. Either the person with responsibility for behaviour issues, or the SENCO, meets with the parents and together they devise an Individual Education Plan for the child. In many early years settings, the child's key worker and other senior management staff may also be involved. If the IEP has been reviewed and there are no significant changes, the second stage can be set in motion.

2 *Early Years Action Plus* or *School Action Plus* is the next stage, when the SENCO or other named person can ask for other agencies to become involved with the child. However, there is still partnership with the parents. Educational psychologists, speech and language therapists, occupational therapists and child and family guidance clinics can be called upon to provide specialised help and support for the child.

3 *Producing a statement of special educational needs* is the last stage of the graduated approach. This is produced by the local educational authority (LEA) following detailed assessments of the child. The LEA seeks information from all of the people, including the parents, who have been involved with the child. The statement clearly identifies the child by name and also includes personal details about their address, date of birth and names and addresses

of their parents. The statement usually reviews the work that has preceded this stage and sets out clear targets to be met through an IEP. Dates for reviews of the IEP and the statement are also included.

The Code of Practice highlights the importance of recognising a child's special educational needs as early as possible and taking appropriate action. This message has been reinforced by the government through the funding of the Early Years Development and Childcare Partnerships (EYDCPs) to support the first two stages and appoint area SENCOs. These SENCOs are able to offer setting-based support, such as developing effective IEPs and staff training, and raising awareness.

Medical or diagnosable conditions that may have a direct influence on behaviour

The term: 'special, individual or particular needs' is used across various settings to describe children who have particular educational needs. These needs could be the result of emotional or behavioural difficulties; or could be the result of a medical or diagnosable condition. Medically related difficulties will be diagnosed by a medical practitioner, and we can work closely with other practitioners; carers; the SENCO etc. to ensure that we are able to provide the best possible environment in which to meet the child's individual needs. This next section considers some of these conditions and gives practical suggestions for helping and empowering children.

Attention Deficit Hyperactivity Disorder (ADHD)

Attention Deficit Hyperactivity Disorder, also referred to as Attention Deficit Disorder (ADD) and hyperkinetic disorder, is a condition that affects between three and five per cent of children and young people. Children with this disorder often find it difficult to sit, to concentrate and may have very high levels of activity compared with children of a similar age. The severity of this disorder varies greatly, with some children displaying only mild symptoms, but for others all aspects of home and school lives are affected.

Recent research into the condition suggests that there are a number of causes including food intolerances, brain damage and genetic factors. Treatment can vary from restricting the diet of the child to the use of very powerful drugs and medications, such as Ritalin. It is generally accepted by medical practitioners that before a child can be diagnosed with ADHD they must show the signs and symptoms at home, and in the school or nursery, for at least six months. It is probable that a child who has no difficulties in one setting, but does in another, has a behavioural difficulty rather than ADHD.

HOW TO HELP A CHILD WITH ADHD

As with the causes, there are many ways in which we can support a child with ADHD. Below are some suggestions, but it is important to remember that every child reacts differently to situations – one strategy may be effective for one child but not for another:

✔ Create a calm atmosphere and remain calm.

✔ Routines and events with structure provide a feeling of security and can help meet the child's need to feel secure and safe.

✔ An awareness of boundaries and 'rules' with regular reminders before an activity can be helpful for older children.

✔ Regular positive feedback for the child on their progress during an activity together with praise and recognition of their achievements can be effective. This could be in the form of stickers and other visual signs of achievement and frequently telling parents and carers about the good and positive aspects of the child.

✔ Try to avoid situations where the child is inactive, or just waiting. Try to keep the child meaningfully occupied, even if it is only with relatively menial tasks, such as setting out a table for a snack or helping an adult.

✔ Try to avoid confrontational situations. For example, try to make activities 'open-ended' so the child can leave them and return, as they need.

✔ Provide situations and activities that can be adult-directed, but in which the child can make choices and decisions and so be empowered.

✔ Acknowledge and praise the child's good behaviour as often as possible.

Remember that other professionals who work in your area, such as educational and medical practitioners, may also be able to give you advice and suggestions.

Autism and Asperger's Syndrome

Autism and Asperger's Syndrome (a form of autism) are developmental disorders specifically affecting three areas of a child's development. These are known as the triad of impairments and are:

◆ communication skills

◆ social interactions

◆ imagination.

They are life-long conditions and children do not grow out of them. Children diagnosed with some form of autism may also have other conditions such as Fragile X syndrome, untreated phenylketonuria and congenital rubella. There are various degrees of severity; at one end of the scale there are those individuals who will never be able to live independently, whilst at the other end, some will be able to lead independent lives but will still have difficulties relating to others.

The number of children with some form of autism is difficult to determine, but it is suggested that about 0.9 per cent of children might be affected. Although the cause is not fully understood more boys than girls are affected, which could suggest a genetic connection. Some current research is looking into the incidence of autism in relation to the MMR vaccine. A medical practitioner or sometimes an educational psychologist usually makes the diagnosis.

HOW TO HELP A CHILD WITH AUTISM

There is no single strategy that can be used, but the National Autistic Society has suggested several approaches that can be used. These include:

- ✔ SPELL
- ✔ TEACCH
- ✔ LOVASS
- ✔ PECS.

Further information can be obtained from the National Autistic Society, whose address and website can be found at the end of the book.

Some children with autism respond well to music therapy, as this can help them to communicate with others.

Other ways to help include:

- ✔ Make sure that you use short sentences that are factual and precise. Don't use unnecessary words, which will only confuse. For example, children with autism do not always understand phrases like 'I'll see' or 'maybe' or 'in a minute'. They need to hear 'yes', 'no' or 'I'll do it now'.
- ✔ Make sure that you have a clear routine and structure to the day, session or activity. If the routine is to change, make sure that you tell the child beforehand in clear and simple language.
- ✔ Try to avoid situations that could cause stress, for example, if the child needs to get dressed in a specific order before going out, allow them the time to do this.
- ✔ Try to create a calm environment or plan a quiet activity, so that the child is not over-stimulated by noise or activities going on around them.
- ✔ Teach the child appropriate ways to relieve their anger and frustrations, such as using a pillow as a punch bag, or screaming into a cushion.

Dyspraxia

Dyspraxia is an impairment of the organisation of movement, and the term replaces such terms as 'clumsy child syndrome'. It is also sometimes referred to as perceptual motor dysfunction, minimal brain dysfunction or motor learning difficulty. The Dyspraxia Foundation estimates that between two and ten per cent of the population could be affected. An educational psychologist usually makes the diagnosis. Children with dyspraxia often become very frustrated and may avoid situations or activities where they believe they cannot succeed. Younger children may find it difficult to sit still for periods of time, as this requires good levels of co-ordination, which they do not have. Some young children may also have difficulties with speech. Older children may be the victims of bullies due to their lack of co-ordination.

HOW TO HELP A CHILD WITH DYSPRAXIA

✔ Provide activities that have structure and repetition especially in relation to the development of physical skills. This will help the child develop movements that may eventually become automatic.

✔ Consider ways of reducing the times that you expect the child to sit still, such as during snack or meal times, circle time or story time.

✔ Use lots of positive reinforcements to encourage and support the child, and be prepared to change the activity to a less demanding one if the child is struggling.

✔ Younger children benefit from activities such as blowing bubbles, which encourages the co-ordination of the mouth muscles.

Fragile X

Fragile X syndrome is an inherited condition and is therefore genetic. It is caused by damage to the X chromosome and because this chromosome is one of the 'gender' chromosomes, it is often said that this syndrome is 'gender-linked'. Females are the carriers of the syndrome, and pass the condition on to their male offspring. Girls can be mildly affected by the condition but boys are often more seriously affected. Children affected by Fragile X syndrome may have developmental delay in several areas; for example, some children have poor communication and speech skills, while other children may have developmental delay with fine and gross motor skills. Some children may also have learning difficulties. Children with Fragile X syndrome may also show autistic tendencies, for example, they may do the same actions repeatedly and may avoid eye contact. Some children may also show signs of ADHD, with poor concentration levels and behaviours that are challenging, such as aggressive outbursts, impulsive actions, irritability and hyperactivity. There are links between Fragile X syndrome and epilepsy with between 10 and 30 per cent of individuals with this syndrome also developing epilepsy.

HOW TO HELP A CHILD WITH FRAGILE X SYNDROME

There is no treatment for this condition and, as the signs and symptoms can vary, it is important to remember that the feelings and needs of the child must be paramount. Some children may be helped by some of the ways outlined for children with ADHD and autism, whereas other children may benefit from speech therapy and some form of concentrated learning support.

✔ Children are not being deliberately aggressive, so make sure that you concentrate on the child and not the aggression.

✔ Plan activities that are short and do not demand long periods of concentration, thus 'setting the child up to fail'.

✔ Many children with this condition are very sociable and may become frustrated that their interactions and communications may not be clear to others. Be a positive role model and help the child to learn by following your example. Play alongside and with the child to provide additional support and help the child to make vital social connections.

✔ Be patient. Allow the child plenty of time to understand and process information. Don't assume that because you have not had a response, the child does not understand; it might just be taking them longer than you anticipated.

Tourette's Syndrome

Tourette's syndrome is a medical condition that affects the nervous system and is inherited. It is estimated that this condition affects 0.2 per cent of the population, and whilst it is inherited, it is also thought that exposure to drugs and other toxins might be contributory factors. Babies who have had difficult births or problems immediately after birth may have a higher risk of developing this syndrome.

Children with this syndrome may suffer from unconscious and involuntary movements and spoken language that are often called tics. These tics can vary in each child and include repetitive eye-blinking or more complex actions such as making unusual facial expressions. Some children may repeat obscene words and phrases, or make socially inappropriate gestures; some repeat phrases that may seem meaningless such as 'you know'. Some children may display several tics at any one time; however, these tics disappear when the child is asleep or concentrating, such as listening to music. Some children become very embarrassed by the tics and by what some people may regard as inappropriate social behaviours. However, the child is not behaving inappropriately deliberately and adults must always acknowledge the feelings of the child and focus on the child rather than on the behaviour. Some children respond to medications such as Haloperidol, while others find relaxation techniques very helpful.

HOW TO HELP A CHILD WITH TOURETTE'S SYNDROME

✔ Focus on the child, be positive and give lots of praise and recognition of achievements and progress.

✔ Help the child to relax perhaps by listening to calming music, focusing on one set of muscles after another (such as the arms) and trying to relax those areas in turn, and by doing breathing exercises.

✔ Behaviour modification plans that offer some reward when the child is able to control a tic may be helpful for some children, but remember that the tics are involuntary.

✔ Help the child to deal and cope with their embarrassment. Some children may become so embarrassed that their stress levels increase, thereby making the tics more pronounced. Again, relaxation techniques and calming environments and activities may help.

Working with outside agencies and other professionals

SENCOs and adults with responsibilities for behaviour management issues can seek advice and support from a wide range of other professionals. In some cases, other professionals may already be involved with a child before they start nursery or school, for example, if the child has a medical problem or sensory impairment.

Primary health care team

Primary health care teams are usually based in the community and are made up of general practitioners, health visitors, community midwives and nurses. All of these professionals work together and are often based in one health centre. Their main aims are treating illness in the community, preventing illness through health education, immunisation programmes and screening, and surveillance programmes. In stable communities where there is not much movement of families, the primary health care team can often establish good relationships with families. It is usually the GP and/or the health visitor who is consulted first if parents have concerns about their child, whether those concerns are about health or behaviour. The health visitor often develops a relationship with the family from when the child is born and sees the children regularly. The health visitor can refer a child and family to the GP or to other professionals. In some communities, health visitors can be supported by a qualified early years worker. These professionals can become involved in a range of activities, such as developing play opportunities, to help parents and children who are giving cause for concern.

CASE STUDY

Beverley gained an NNEB qualification in 1996 and began her professional career in a day nursery. Two years later she moved to a primary school, where she worked alongside a small group of children with learning and behavioural difficulties in Years 3 and 4. In 2000 she joined a primary health care team, working mainly with one health visitor. Her work involved visiting families in their homes and advising parents about immunisation and surveillance programmes. Beverley helped parents develop play opportunities, particularly in families where the health visitor had identified children who were not thriving. Beverley also established a crèche facility at the health centre during antenatal clinics.

1   How do you think Beverley's work experiences in a day nursery might help her in her present role?

2   Working with children with learning and behavioural difficulties requires a lot of patience and good communication skills. How might these attributes help Beverley as part of the primary health care team?

School health services

The responsibility for health surveillance moves to the school health team once a child starts school. The team is made up of school nurses, dentists and doctors. Children have regular dental, hearing and sight checks and the immunisation programme is continued. In some areas, however, the school health service has been reduced due to financial constraints and in such circumstances the responsibilities remain with the primary health care team.

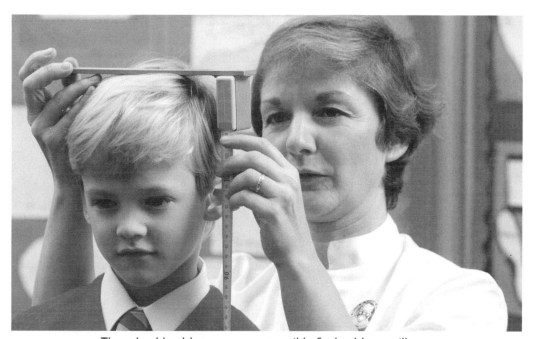

The school health team are responsible for health surveillance

Sure Start

Sure Start aims to improve the health and well-being of families and children both before and after birth, so children are ready to flourish when they go to school. In many areas, Sure Start teams form part of the primary health care team. Sure Start is a cornerstone of the government's drive to tackle child poverty and social exclusion and it is anticipated that by 2004 there will be at least 500 Sure Start local programmes. These will be concentrated in communities and neighbourhoods where a high proportion of children are living in poverty. Sure Start aims to allow parents, parents-to-be and children to access support, advice on nurturing, health services and early learning. All Sure Start programmes work with their Early Years Development and Childcare Partnerships (EYDCP) to help close the gap between the availability of accessible childcare for 0–3 year olds in Sure Start areas. This can be achieved by Sure Start staff taking children to pre-school groups and supporting the staff in those groups in offering appropriate learning experiences to the children. Sure Start staff can seek advice and support from other professionals and access the services of other childcare professionals, such as therapists and paediatricians, if necessary.

CASE STUDY

A Sure Start team in north-west England includes experienced and qualified childcare and education workers. These practitioners go to families where the children are failing to thrive and often have poor social skills. In one family the health visitor had concerns about a three-year-old who was not talking and rarely went out. One member of the Sure Start team, Ravi, started to visit the child at home regularly and play with him. After a few weeks Ravi took the mother and the child to a local supermarket and gradually began to develop the confidence of both mother and child. After a few months it was suggested that the child should join a pre-school group supported by Ravi. The child was collected by Ravi and taken to a local group. Ravi stayed with the child for the first three weeks and gradually began to reduce the time she stayed at the playgroup. By the time the child was due to start school he had started talking and was confident enough to mix with other children. Contact with the family was maintained, as by now another child had been born, and it was shown that the first child was making good progress at school and coping well.

1 Describe the steps that Ravi took to gradually develop the child's social skills.

2 Why do you think it was important to maintain contact with the family?

3 One of Sure Start's national objectives is to improve children's ability to learn. How do you think Ravi met this objective?

Family centres

Family centres are set up by local social services departments, often working with the local education authority. In some areas Sure Start has also become involved with family centres. Family centres aim to provide support, advice, guidance and practical help for parents, so that they can learn how to identify and meet the needs of their children. Family centres often have many professionals available to offer help and advice, such as a play therapist, health visitors and counsellors. Families are usually referred to the family centre by the primary health care team, but many will also become involved with families who are referred by teachers, social workers and therapists. Many centres offer crèche facilities whilst parents attend parenting courses or other activities. Some also operate toy libraries, drop-in centres and contact centres, where parents can have supervised access to their children following court procedures.

Other professionals

The following table looks at the role of some of the other professionals who work with children with behavioural difficulties. This list is not complete as some children with specific conditions, such as Tourette's syndrome or sickle cell anaemia, may be referred to a medical specialist, in the same way that children displaying inappropriate behaviour as a result of a family problem, such as alcohol or drug abuse, may be referred to a specialist in that area.

Professional	Role	When they get involved
Social worker	Works with children in need, including children with behavioural issues if the family is experiencing difficulties.	Becomes involved with families if child abuse is suspected, or if there is a child with a severe disability. Can offer advice about benefits and childcare. Can liaise with other organisations, such as government departments for social security, education and health.
Educational psychologist	Specialises in the way children learn, carrying out diagnostic tests on children's cognitive and language development.	Often the first professional to be consulted by nurseries and schools as part of the second stage Code of practice. Works closely with them to offer support and advice on how to meet the needs of all the children, particularly those who are cause for concern.
Clinical psychologist	Mostly hospital-based, works with individuals of all ages who have inappropriate behaviour patterns, to plan and develop programmes of behaviour modification or therapy.	Referal by the primary health care team or an educational psychologist, and their recommendations are implemented by the child's family and nursery/school. May become involved as part of the procedures of the Code of Practice, but more likely involved as a result of the statementing stage.

Professional	Role	When they get involved
Paediatrician	A specialist doctor, usually hospital-based, focusing on the treatment and care of sick children.	Referal by a GP or the primary health care team.
Child psychiatrist	A specialist doctor, focusing on the treatment and care of children with mental illnesses.	Works with a child and their family to try and find out what the child is feeling and thinking.
Speech and language therapist	Works with people of all ages, based in hospitals, community family centres and community medical centres. Specialises in any kind of speech or language delay, or communication disorder. Carries out a diagnostic assessment, before planning and developing exercises to help the individual.	Referal by the primary health care team. The exercises are designed so that parents, nursery and school staff can carry them out with the child.
Play and music therapists	Music therapists work with all ages, but play therapists work primarily with children. Often employed by hospitals on children's wards. Use toys and props to help children in difficult situations or with behavioural difficulties, to develop other ways of expressing strong emotions such as anger or grief.	Referal by the primary health care team. It has been proved that play therapy speeds up the recovery process for many children Therefore it is used, for example, when a child is in a frightening or disturbing situation, such as during a hospital stay, in order to help the child express what they do not have the vocabulary to articulate.
Occupational therapist	Involved with children with physical disabilities. Often based in hospitals, but can undertake home visits, to offer, for example, advice on adaptations to the home environment and the use of suitable equipment for the child.	Can visit nurseries and schools as well as homes, to advise how children with physical disabilities can be encouraged to be as independent as possible.
Physiotherapist	Usually hospital-based, but can treat people in community health centres. Works with people of all ages with physical problems that have been caused by accidents, illness or ageing. Devises, exercises for children with physical difficulties, aiming to develop and strengthen muscles.	The devised exercises can be carried out at home, school or nursery.

Gemma is the key worker for Thomas, and she has to attend the six month review meeting with his parents, his teacher, social worker and the educational psychologist. The meeting has been arranged for 4.00 pm. As Gemma is about to leave school her colleague stops for a chat, as a result Gemma misses the bus and arrives late. In her rush she has forgotten to bring the observations that she has carried out on Thomas. Thomas' social worker accuses her of being uncaring and not interested in the child. He says that Gemma shows little understanding of Thomas' difficulties and that someone else should be his key worker.

1 What mistakes has Gemma made in establishing a good relationship with the other professionals and Thomas' parents?

2 Do you think that Thomas' social worker was right in his assumptions about Gemma?

3 If you were Gemma, what would you do next?

Developing successful working relationships with other professionals

Many childcare and education workers say that they feel 'in awe' of other professionals and lack confidence when dealing with them. This can be especially true when the other professional appears to be better 'qualified' than the childcare and education worker. However, it is important to remember that you both have the best interests of the child and his or her family at heart. This gives you common ground, a starting point on which to build your relationship.

There are several things that you can do to make sure that any relationships that you develop with other professionals are sound, effective and will ultimately benefit the child.

◆ **Be professional.** Present yourself and your work with the child in a business-like way and appear confident. This can include simple things like your appearance; first impressions do count and if you appear tidy and appropriately dressed, other professionals will notice. If, on the other hand, your clothes are untidy or inappropriate for the situation, you could give the impression of someone who does not care.

It is important to have a neat and tidy appearance

◆ **Share information**. You have valuable information to share about the child since the other professionals do not know the child as well as you. It is important that this information is presented accurately and factually. Use your records and observation details if appropriate. Do not try to give the impression that you know more than you actually do – stick to the facts and the evidence.

◆ When attending meetings where you are asked to contribute, it is a good idea to **make notes beforehand**. Take the time to think about what you are going to say, how you will say it, and use your notes to make sure that you do not forget to mention any important and relevant information. Remember to maintain issues of confidentiality at all times.

◆ **Avoid using jargon**. All professionals have a 'specialist vocabulary' which is perfectly acceptable with people of the same profession. However, it is not necessary to use jargon as it may not be fully understood by others outside the profession. This can lead to ambiguities and misunderstandings. Another form of jargon can be to use initial letters for complete words, such as ELGs for Early Learning Goals, and ADHD for attention deficit and hyperactivity disorder. *You* know what you are talking about, but a social worker may not. It is good practice to use clear plain language. If someone you are with uses jargon or initials, and you do not know what they mean, ask. It is far better to ask a sensible question to gain information than pretend that you understand when you don't.

◆ Take positive steps to **improve your own communication skills**. This not only helps you to develop successful relationships with other professionals but also helps when working with parents and their children. Communication that is effective is the key to any successful relationship. Communication skills are discussed in more detail in Chapter 10.

ACTIVITY

Imagine that you are a classroom assistant working with a small group of six-year-old children who have behavioural difficulties. You have been asked to attend a review of their IEPs with the teacher, parents and educational psychologists. Rewrite the following extracts of information to provide factual evidence for the meeting:

a Connor frequently hits other children, especially at lunchtime.

b Matthew drives me and the teacher mad as he is very difficult to control.

c Priya is spoilt and wants her own way all of the time, when she doesn't get it she has a temper tantrum.

Working in pre-school settings

The pre-school group, including parents/carer and toddler sessions may be the first place outside the family where a child will meet other children of a similar age. These groups can be invaluable as they provide company, support and opportunities for sharing concerns and worries.

Many pre-school groups are managed by a committee made up of parents and other interested individuals, and sometimes the play leader or supervisor. The groups must be staffed by appropriately qualified adults, who are often supported and assisted by volunteer helpers. These helpers are usually parents of children in the group and it is not uncommon for their children to behave inappropriately when it is their parents who are helping. It is very important that volunteer helpers understand and implement the agreed behaviour policy of the group if their child, or any other, behaves in an inappropriate way.

The teams working in these groups, in England, must ensure that their settings meet the National Standards for Under Eights – Day Care and Child Minding (2001), and they are inspected by OFSTED (CSIW in Wales). Standard 11 of the National Standards relates to children's behaviour and its main focus is that adults have a consistent and positive approach to behaviour management. The groups develop behaviour policies and often have a SENCO. All of the group's policies should be shared with each parent and carer. The Pre-School Learning Alliance produces exemplar policies that teams can use to develop their own policy.

Groups have access to all of the other services and professional advice and an increasing number are involved in Sure Start programmes, which enable parents, carers and staff to access family support services, health services and early learning activities and events.

Encouraging positive behaviour

One way of encouraging positive behaviour is for staff to create an environment that is safe for children and one in which they are not being repeatedly told *not* to do things. Many pre-school groups meet in shared premises (such as a church hall) and sometimes have little control over the physical environment in which the children play and learn. However, there are positive things that staff can do, for example:

◆ arrange the room so that all areas and activities can be seen by staff

◆ use moveable furniture to create specific areas and control children's movements around the room

◆ consider placing activities that require concentration, such as small construction, at one end of the room, with vigorous play, such as an indoor climbing frame, at the other end. This will prevent children from disturbing each other. Alternatively, an activities rota could be used, with 'quiet' activities being cleared away before larger play equipment is set up and trikes are brought out.

Working in day nurseries/day care

As with pre-school groups and other forms of sessional day care, nurseries are inspected by OFSTED and have to meet the requirements of Standard 11. Many nurseries have responsibilities towards young children for up to ten hours a day and often for five days a week. As a result, children come into contact with several staff, both qualified and unqualified, during the course of a day, even with an effective key worker system. It is essential therefore that nurseries have workable set procedures that guide their practice and ensure a consistent approach. Nurseries have a named person who has overall responsibility for behaviour management issues, a SENCO, and this individual should have the skills and appropriate training to support other staff and access advice and

Team work is very important in all settings

guidance from other professionals. Nurseries need to have a written record of significant incidences of inappropriate behaviour. This record should be read and signed by both the staff member involved and the parent/carer of the child.

Nurseries also find it useful to use individual education plans for some children (see page 142). Many nurseries devise such plans for all children, not just those whose behaviour is causing concern. The IEPs are often developed by key workers, or in the case of behavioural concerns, the SENCO.

Teamwork is very important in day nurseries and day care settings. Many day nurseries have staff who work with one particular age group, such as babies or toddlers, so small teams are part of the organisation of the setting. However, all the staff are part of the overall nursery team and as such have responsibilities to support each other, share experiences and skills and make collective decisions.

SNAPSHOT

Kelly is the baby room supervisor in a 56-place day nursery, with a team of eight other staff members. Kelly and the rest of the team are also key workers for two babies each. Each key worker has responsibility to make sure that the home/nursery diary is completed for each baby at the end of the session. One member of the team has very good art and creative skills, so she has responsibility for displays in the baby room. Another team member has taken a counselling course at the local college and her skills are put to good use throughout the nursery. All the staff in the baby room have been involved in the development of a policy to promote positive behaviour and make sure that they implement it consistently with all of the children.

Encouraging positive behaviour

Nurseries can encourage positive behaviour by developing and establishing a **routine** to the day. This helps children to feel secure and to develop an understanding of what is going to happen throughout the day. All routines must be flexible in order to meet individual children's needs, allowing a certain amount of freedom of choice to cope with unexpected events. However, the overarching framework or pattern of the day is predictable.

It has been shown that many incidences of inappropriate behaviour happen because children are confined in a small space. It is therefore important to consider the children's **environment**. Children may become irritable when their movements and play are curbed, and many childcare professionals report distinct changes in patterns of behaviour at times. Nurseries should make sure that children have frequent opportunities to take part in vigorous and physical play, preferably outside. The weather is frequently used as an excuse not to go outside; but often there is no reason why children can't play outside when it is cold or raining providing that they are adequately dressed and supervised. If children and staff really can't go outside at some time during the day, consider moving the children around the nursery to a different room for a physical play activity.

It is also important that there are sufficient toys and equipment for the children to play with. It is very difficult to encourage children to share and co-operate if there are insufficient resources.

Although nurseries must have a named person, a SENCO, with responsibility for behaviour management issues, this does not mean that one individual has sole responsibility for producing a policy. As with pre-school groups, all staff, including domestic and administrative staff, should be involved. The views of children should also be taken into account. No nursery has the same policy, as the needs of both the children and staff are different from one nursery to the next. There are exemplar policies and statements available that can be useful starting points for developing a policy, especially where staff may feel that they do not have the experience or skills necessary. The policy should be shared with parents and children, and be open to discussion and regular review.

Many nurseries also include in their policy the role of the adult in encouraging positive behaviour. This can be very helpful when new staff are employed and when students undertake training. The role of the adult may include points such as:

◆ All adults must implement the policy consistently at all times.

◆ All adults should avoid harming a child's self-esteem, by using inappropriate methods for behaviour management such as humiliation, segregation, using a 'naughty' chair or corner, or withholding food.

◆ Adults should not discuss children's behaviour with other staff or parents in front of them or others.

◆ All adults should appreciate that children are learning to deal with a wide range of emotions and feelings and at times will need help and support in order to cope with these experiences.

Working in schools, including nursery classes

Schools have a named person who has been identified as the Special Educational Needs Co-ordinator (SENCO), but may not necessarily have one person who has the responsibility specifically for behaviour management. More often than not, the SENCO has this responsibility as many behaviour difficulties are the result of, or part of, a child's special educational needs. In many cases children who have difficulties managing their behaviour in nursery have their details passed to the SENCO of the next school, particularly if the difficulties are affecting their learning.

Most children make the transition from nursery or pre-school group without any problems. Many settings have clear and positive policies and guidelines to introduce children gradually into their new environment; however, some children still experience problems adjusting to the differences in numbers and can be overwhelmed. In most nurseries children are cared for in small groups with an adult-to-child ratio of 1 to 8 for children between three and seven years old. In schools, children are usually in large groups with one teacher and possibly an assistant. Class sizes vary greatly across the country and may be as large as 30 or more or as low as 20.

Encouraging positive behaviour

All schools have a duty to state and pursue policies designed to promote positive behaviour and discipline. Children come into school with a wide range of experiences. There is a danger that adults in schools will make assumptions about a child's behaviour based on previous knowledge of the family. This may lead to a self-fulfilling prophecy about the way a child might behave. It is also taking an unhelpful stereotypical standpoint and will do little to promote positive behaviour.

Some children in school may be only four years old and may find the school day exhausting. Children are expected to be more independent than in pre-school or nursery; they are expected to move around the buildings in ways that do not distract or interfere with other children. The school day is likely to be more structured with larger group activities, which require children to listen to the teacher. Children therefore need adult support and positive role models, from both the adults and the other children, if they are going to manage their own behaviour successfully.

As with pre-schools and nurseries, positive behaviour can be encouraged through the arrangement of the physical environment. These might be relatively simple things, such as making sure quiet activities that require concentration do not take place near a more noisy activity, and providing frequent opportunities to 'let off steam' and engage in physical and vigorous play. Children need the structure of a routine in order to meet their need for security and help them become more confident and independent.

Schools have a behaviour policy that clearly sets out the procedures and expectations regarding behaviour. As with all other settings, it is very important that this policy is implemented in a consistent manner. Schools and other early years settings can seek advice from other professionals if the usual strategies and procedures in the policy are not having an impact on managing a child's behaviour. In extreme cases a child can be excluded from a school and there should be clear criteria and procedures that must be followed, not only for the exclusion but also for the reintegration of the child into the school.

Most schools have a policy to deal with **bullying**. Some schools have this as a separate policy or as part of their overall behaviour management policy.

Many of the issues involved with developing an effective behaviour management policy can be addressed by incorporating them into citizenship lessons. Citizenship is now compulsory in secondary schools, and many primary schools have already incorporated aspects of the citizenship curriculum into their personal, social and health education programmes. Children as young as those in Year 1 can be presented with role-plays and scenarios where they can act out and consider issues relating to behaviour in non-threatening situations.

ACTIVITY FOR YEARS 1 AND 2

Consider the following scenario, based on a fictional newspaper report.

MUGGER, AGED 5, ESCAPES PROSECUTION

A child believed to be the youngest mugger in the country cannot be dealt with by the police because he is only five years old. He and his eight-year-old friend were seen attacking an elderly woman in the high street. The boys were trying to grab her bag. The incident happened last Saturday at 2 pm and was seen by the Patel family who were out shopping. Mrs Patel went to help the old lady whilst Mr Patel and his son held on to the two boys. Mr Patel phoned the police on his mobile phone. 'The lads didn't seem to be bothered at all by what they had done and kept shouting and swearing at us, even when the police arrived,' said Mrs Patel. 'I asked them how they would feel if the old lady was their granny, but they said they didn't care.' The police took the boys to the police station, but had to let them go as they were both under ten. Mrs Patel said that she thought it was terrible that these children could get away with such behaviour.

Ask the following questions to encourage discussion and get children thinking about unacceptable behaviour.

1 What do you think the boys had done wrong?

2 Do you think that Mr and Mrs Patel were right to phone the police?

3 Why do you think the boys were not bothered about what they had done?

4 How do you think the boys should be dealt with?

Working in play schemes, before- and after-school clubs

In all of these settings, teamwork is important. Play workers, as other professionals, have a variety of skills and talents that can be used to benefit the whole team. For example, one play worker may be a skilled footballer, another particularly creative and another very musical. All of these talents can be used to enrich the play experiences of the children. In these settings the emphasis is on play, with the minimum of restrictions on the children. Many play workers would advocate that children need a certain level of risk in order to extend and develop their experiences; that does not mean, however, that their safety and well-being should be compromised. Many play settings work with children to develop a set of standards that are considered acceptable. Part of the first assumption of Playwork states, 'children's play is freely chosen, personally directed behaviour, motivated from within', and children are encouraged to develop their own ground rules.

CASE STUDY

At an after-school club attached to a primary school the children discussed the ground rules with the staff and eventually decided on only one:

We will play with everyone in ways that we would want them to play with us.

The children and staff worked on the idea of the 'marble in the jar', with everybody consistently sticking to the ground rule of putting a marble in a jar. Those that didn't follow the ground rule would find a marble had been removed. When the jar was full everyone decided upon a treat.

1 How do you think this 'rule' would work in your setting?

2 How do you think you could adapt the 'marble in a jar' idea for your settling?

Working in a private home

Practitioners in this situation are likely to be childminders and nannies, not forgetting of course parents and carers, including foster carers. Many people working in such situations may not consider themselves part of a team, but this is not true. All childminders and nannies must work in partnership with a child's parents and carers, and this is teamwork. In the same way, parents and carers should work in partnership with a child's teachers and other professionals. In many areas childminding networks are being established, and these provide excellent opportunities for childminders to work in teams and share experiences and expertise. Many private nannies can join informal groups of people employed in similar positions and can share experiences, skills and expertise.

House rules, behaviour policies or statements may not be formally written down in such settings, especially for parents, but are understood by all concerned. Many childminders do, however, include a written statement in their welcome packs on behaviour. This makes sure that parents and carers clearly understand how the childminder will promote positive behaviour and manage any incidences of inappropriate behaviour. This will also ensure that there is a consistent approach and teamwork. Many nannies and parents work together with the children to establish house rules that can be consistently applied.

Childminders, nannies and parents and carers can seek additional support from other professionals. This is often accessed through the child's health visitor, doctor or through voluntary agencies and support groups, such as an ADHD or breavement support group.

CHECKPOINT

1 List four key features of an effective team.

2 What do the letters SENCO stand for?

3 How many stages are there in the Code of Practice for the Identification and Assessment of Children with Special Educational Needs?

4 Which professionals would you normally expect to find in a primary health care team?

5 What does Sure Start aim to do?

6 Family centres are independent organisations: true or false?

7 What does an educational psychologist specialise in?

8 What is the main role of a clinical psychologist?

9 What implications do the National Standards for Under Eights Day Care and Childminding have for managing children's behaviour?

Chapter 10

Communicating with parents and carers

Introduction

Parents and primary carers, such as close relatives or foster carers, are the most important people in a young child's life. They are the child's first teachers and educators and can powerfully influence their attitudes and all aspects of their development. It is from them that children learn about their family's culture and religious beliefs. It is vital that any individual working with other people's children makes every effort to work in partnership with parents and carers. It is essential that this partnership is built on mutual trust, respect and understanding.

A partnership is a joint venture that should aim to meet a child's needs, with both the setting and the parents working together. Partnerships do not just happen; they need to be developed with care and thought. Some parents find it hard to accept that the behaviour of their child may not always be appropriate, or that their child is difficult to manage. Parents are naturally very emotionally involved with their child and this can sometimes cloud their judgements. The ability to relate to and work in partnership with parents is a crucial part of the role of a professional childcare worker. This is especially important when promoting positive behaviour and managing children's inappropriate behaviour.

It is important that we can communicate effectively with parents and carers as well as other professionals who may be involved in offering support to the child and their family.

This chapter will look at:

◆ the rights of parents
◆ different styles of parenting and family structures
◆ parents and carers as partners
◆ communication skills.

The rights of parents

In recent years there have been positive changes in attitudes towards parents' rights, especially in the education and care of their children. The United Nations Convention on the Rights of the Child acknowledges the rights of parents, affirming that the state must respect the rights and responsibilities of parents and the extended family to provide guidance for the child that is appropriate to her or his evolving capabilities. It goes on to say that parents have primary responsibility for raising their child and the state shall support them in this. The Convention also states that a child has a right to live with his or her parents provided that this is in the child's best interests, and that the child has a right to maintain contact with both parents if separated from one or both.

The Children Act 1989

The Children Act 1989 gave parents definite rights, such as being able to express a preference about which school their child should attend. According to the Act, local authorities and other agencies and services have to work with parents to support them and make separation from parents the last option. The Children Act also introduced the concept of parental responsibility to promote the idea that parents have 'responsibilities' towards their children. The term is defined as

> 'all rights, duties, powers, responsibilities and authority which by law a parent of a child has in relation to that child or his property.'
> © Crown copyright

When a couple is not married, only the mother automatically acquires parental responsibility. An unmarried father needs to secure parental responsibility by agreement with the mother or by order of the Court. Carers, such as close relatives, can be given parental responsibility if it is considered to be in the child's best interests, such as grandparents who have been granted a residence order. A local authority, when given a care order for a child, shares parental responsibility with the natural parents. Parental responsibility remains with a parent, or other appropriate person, until the child is 18 years old, even if the child is no longer living with them.

Parental responsibilities include the right to:

◆ choose the religion of the child
◆ choose where the child should live
◆ choose a name for the child and to register their birth

- protect and look after the child
- consent to medical treatment on behalf of the child
- make sure that their child is in full-time education between the ages of five and sixteen years
- apply for a passport for the child
- appoint a legal guardian.

National Standards for the Regulation of Day Care and Childminding

In 2002, the National Standards for the Regulation of Day Care and Childminding in England were incorporated into the Children Act under the new Part XA. There are fourteen National Standards that all providers of childcare and childminders of children under the age of eight are required to comply with. Standard 12 is 'Working in Partnership with Parents and Carers'. Settings are required to work with parents to ensure that the needs of the child are met, both individually and as a group, and that information is shared. Most early years settings and schools had already developed policies, or had written statements that aimed to make parents partners in the care and education of their child. The National Standards formalised this idea and clearly set out what settings and early years establishments should do in order to work in partnership with parents.

Early years settings are required to give parents accessible information, for example, in Braille or different languages. Policies should be available to parents, and any personal information on children and their families must be stored securely, with privacy and confidentiality a priority. Parents have the right to have access to any records that are kept about their children. It is good practice to explain to parents why records are kept and what use will be made of the information. Many settings include this information in their prospectus or brochure, and some tell parents at their initial meeting or as part of the settling-in policy. Settings need to have parental agreement before information can be shared with other professionals; however, when a child is considered to be at risk, or in need of protection, information can be passed on to referring agencies without the consent of parents.

THINK IT OVER:

- Who else might need to see records about a child who is displaying inappropriate behaviour?
- How can parents access information about their child without seeing those of other children?
- What information should be kept in children's records and how should staff write them? How might this impact on parents and the partnership?

Different styles of parenting

Parents do not always choose how they bring up their children or how they influence their learning and behaviour. Most parents are influenced by their own upbringing and the way that their own parents dealt with them. The pressures of daily life, the environment, their culture, religion and family structures also affect parenting styles (see Chapter 1). Most parents want the best for their children, and love and care for them, but the way in which they do this varies enormously. Many parenting styles are perhaps not perfect or exemplary, but usually provide children with consistency, care and love.

Generally there are three main styles of parenting, although there can be overlap between each style:

1   **Permissive** – permissive parents allow their children lots of personal choice and responsibility. They may not make attempts to manage the behaviour of the children. This style can perhaps be summed up by the phrase 'He/she will learn from his/her own mistakes.'

2   **Authoritarian** – authoritarian parents are the opposite of permissive parents. They attempt to manage, control and limit the behaviour of their children. They may spend time explaining 'rules' and boundaries and may have high expectations of their children. This style can perhaps be summed up by the phrase 'You must do it because I say so.'

3   **Authoritative** – this is the most common style of parenting. Such parents try to manage their children's behaviour; they listen to their children as well as explaining the reasons for certain limits or rules. This style can be summed up by the phrase, 'If you continue to argue with your brother over that toy, I will take it away.'

A study by **E. Maccoby and J. Martin** in 1983 looked at the personalities of parents and how this influenced and affected the development of children. The studies differentiated between the warm and friendly personality traits of parents and those who could be described as having aggressive, cold and hostile personality characteristics. It was found that warm parents express affection and care for their children, often putting their needs before their own. They respond with understanding and compassion to their children's needs. Warm parents are interested in and enthusiastic about their children's schooling, activities and experiences. Their children develop secure attachments and have good levels of self-esteem. On the other hand, children of hostile parents may feel rejected, may have low self-esteem and may not be able to develop secure attachments and meaningful relationships. Their parents may show their feelings in actions, words and behaviour, showing that they do not love their children and/or are not interested in them. In such cases, the needs of the children may not be fully met.

It is very important, if early years professionals and parents are to work in partnership, that there is respect for the parenting style. There is no 'correct' parenting style and early years professionals should avoid making stereotypical assumptions about a child or their parents based on the parenting style.

Different family structures

There are a wide variety of family structures in Western society today. Although the traditional structure of a family composed of two parents of the opposite sex being married with children is the norm still, this is being challenged by a rapid rise in different practices. The main family structures are shown in the chart below.

Family structure	Main features	Example
Adoptive family	Children are not living with their birth parents but have been legally adopted.	Some couples who are unable to have children for medical reasons may choose to adopt.
Extended family	Common in many parts of the world and was the traditional structure for centuries in the United Kingdom.	Three, or sometimes four, generations of the same family live close together. Grandparents and other relatives may help to care for the children.
Homosexual/lesbian family	Children live with one natural parent and a same sex step-parent.	A pair of gay men made headline news in 2001 when they adopted twin girls, to 'make their family complete.'
Mixed ethnic background	Parents hold different religious beliefs or are from a different ethnic group.	The media personalities Dawn French and Lenny Henry and their daughter could be described as having a mixed ethnic family structure.
Nomadic family	The families do not stay in one place for very long, but are often surrounded by other family members.	Travellers and gypsies, or fairground people.
Nuclear	The 'traditional family'. Parents have the responsibility of caring for their children.	Often portrayed as a 'normal' family structure; made up of two married parents and two children.
Reconstituted family	One natural parent and one step-parent.	Children can be described as 'yours', 'mine' and 'ours'.
Single-parent family	One natural parent, of either sex, cares for the children on their own.	Can be as a result of divorce, separation, death of a partner, or in some cases a single woman who has elected to have a child.
Communal families	Several, sometimes unrelated family groups, choose to live together and share the responsibilities of childcare.	In Israel, communes called kibbutzim provide an extended family for children who can be effectively cared for by adults other than their parents or immediate family.

Different types of family structures

ACTIVITY

Think about your own upbringing and answer the following questions.

◆ Did your parent/s say what time you had to be back home by in the evenings?

◆ Did they limit the number of nights that you were allowed out as a teenager?

◆ Did you know what the consequences would be if you 'broke' the rules?

◆ How have these experiences influenced your views on parenting?

◆ How has your upbringing influenced the ways you manage inappropriate behaviour and promote positive behaviour?

Cultural variations in family structures and parenting styles

In the late 1980s, studies in America, undertaken by **Beatrice Whiting** and **Carolyn Edwards**, compared the variations of parenting in such diverse societies as urban America, rural Kenya and Liberia. The studies showed that there were many overarching similarities, despite the vast differences in economic, social and political conditions. With infants and toddlers, the universal emphasis was on providing routine care along with attention and support. By the time the child reached four years of age, most parents shifted their focus to controlling, correcting or managing inappropriate behaviour. Finally, when children reached the age for formal schooling, parents become concerned with training their children in the skills and social behaviour valued by their cultural group.

There were also notable differences, for example, mothers from rural villages in Kenya and Liberia focused on training their children to do work and placed a high premium on obedience. As soon as children were physically able, their mothers delegated some of their heavy workloads to the children, such as caring for the family's animals, working in the fields and caring for younger siblings. Children were rarely praised and unconventional behaviours were not tolerated. In the American families it was noted that mothers and children interacted and talked a great deal; mothers were liberal in their use of praise and encouragement and firm training, and heavy disciplinary techniques were not part of their parenting style. The study concluded that parents around the world resemble each other in numerous ways because of the universal needs of children as they grow and develop.

How parents manage their children's behaviour

How parents manage their children's behaviour in order to meet their needs varies and is affected by many factors. These influences do not necessarily affect how successful the parents are at managing.

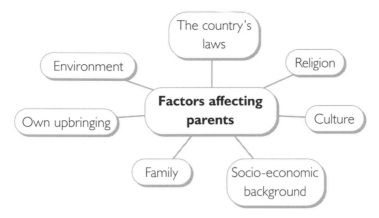

Parents are influenced by different factors

A country's laws may determine how parents teach their children acceptable behaviour; for example, stealing is an offence in the United Kingdom and therefore most parents teach their children not to steal. Family expectations of how members should behave also affect parents and their children. For example, it may be an 'unwritten rule' that children must not disagree with their grandparents, or that they must be 'nice ' to their cousins.

The socio-economic background of an individual may affect their vocabulary and how they react and behave in some situations. Children learn from their parents' patterns of speech and behaviour what the 'norms' are for their group. It must be remembered that socio-economic class differences are not as pronounced in Western societies as they once were, but in some societies socio-economic class is still a strong influencing factor.

Religion may be a powerful influence on how parents manage their children. Some religions have strict codes of conduct or rules that their followers live by, such as forms of dress and what to eat. Culture may also be a powerful influence on parents and children; for example, Japanese parents rarely use physical punishment.

Parents as partners in the care and education of their children

For many years it was considered that the 'professionals' knew best when it came to matters of childcare and education. Parents often felt unwelcome or uncomfortable in a setting and many thought that their views were not important. However, this attitude has virtually disappeared and it is now recognised that children benefit when their parents and carers, and/or teachers work together

Getting the partnership started

Many early years professionals fully recognise and acknowledge that parents are the main source of information about their child, not just when the child starts at the setting but throughout their time at school or nursery. We are all influenced by first impressions. We look at how someone is dressed, or the way that they speak, and make a judgement, rightly or wrongly, about what sort of person they might be. This makes the initial meeting with parents one of the most important that practitioners may have. They need to try to make sure that the first meeting goes as well as possible since the chances of building a successful partnership are significantly reduced if there are initial problems. It is very important that childcare workers do not make judgements about parents based on preconceived and stereotypical opinions, such as why parents wish to have someone else care for their child, or how they speak or dress. If a parent thinks that the staff at the setting disapprove of their lifestyle, it will affect the quality of the partnership.

The initial meeting

The initial meeting should be a mutual exchange of information – a partnership from the start. Information needs to be exchanged about the child's needs, the parents' needs, the setting's requirements, and important contact details. Many settings provide a prospectus or brochure that they can give to parents to read in their own time, but this is no substitute for personal interactions and contact.

CASE STUDY

Edward is nearly three years old and about to start at the local pre-school group. He has never been cared for by anyone other than his parents and grandparents. His mother is quite concerned about leaving him as she feels that he is shy and can be 'clingy'. Edward and his mother are invited to the end-of-term party with other new children, as part of the group's settling-in policy. Edward spends most of the time sitting on his mother's knee, with his face buried in her shoulder. At the start of term, Edward and his mother attend the group together for the first hour, then gradually the time that they spend together is decreased, while the time that Edward spends at the group is increased. After about three weeks, Edward, who is still a bit 'clingy' when his mother leaves, settles and participates in all of the group's activities. Edward's mother knows who his key worker is and talks to her each time Edward attends the group.

1   How do you think the settling-in policy helped Edward?

2   What do you think are the positive features of this setting's policy?

3   How do you think Edward's key worker could develop the relationship with his mother?

The initial meeting is very important for child, parent and staff

Many settings have a settling-in policy where a child is gradually introduced into the group with their parents. In this way, both the parents and child get to know the expectations for behaviour together and this helps to develop a consistent approach.

Establishing positive communications at the outset

At the beginning of a partnership with parents it is important that staff establish how the parent wishes to be addressed. Some parents may be quite happy for staff to use their first name, while others may wish to be addressed using their title, such as Mrs Patel or Dr Webb. All staff should always remember that children may not always have the same family name as both of their parents; if in doubt, ask. Names are important and parents and children should be greeted with their correct names every time they come to the setting. The chances of a partnership between parents and staff succeeding are greatly improved when positive communications are established early on.

Working together to manage children's behaviour takes time and effort. There may be times when the only things staff say to parents about their child are negative comments. This can be detrimental to the partnership and whilst staff should always be truthful it is good practice to make a positive comment about a child. Even the most difficult child will usually have done something appropriate, such as hanging up their coat, eating all of their lunch or getting to the end of an activity.

Developing the partnership

Many settings and establishments not only have regular meetings between parents and carers, but also operate an 'open door' policy which gives parents the opportunity to talk to staff about their child whenever they feel there is a need. Parents do not need to wait for an appointment if they have a concern about their child. There may not be time for a full and frank discussion at the first approach, but the open door policy makes it possible for further meetings to be arranged to suit both parents and staff. It is a two-way process, from which children, parents and staff can benefit. This policy helps develop a sense of trust between parents and staff, a strong relationship between parents and carers, and helps link home and school experiences for the child. Children realise that all the important people in their lives are working together and this helps meet their needs for security and belonging.

Involving parents in the setting

Many settings involve parents as voluntary helpers. Parents may have many skills and areas of expertise that they can share with staff and children, for example, a parent who is a dentist could talk to the children about dental hygiene, or a grandparent could talk about the toys that they played with when they were children. Settings must make sure that all helpers feel valued and respected and that they do not just do the 'rotten' jobs that no one else wants, such as washing out the paint pots! It is important that this aspect of the partnership is handled well; parents and carers need clear, explicit guidelines about their role and responsibilities.

At the same time, it must be remembered that helpers are volunteers and presumably have come to help because they *want* to; therefore the experience should be enjoyable. They could be worried that they may do something wrong or that their child will behave in inappropriate ways. All parents should understand the behaviour policy of the setting and be prepared to implement it, if necessary. The helper's child should not be allowed to behave any differently to the other children. If this does happen, then it would perhaps be a good idea to suggest to the parent that they help children in a different area, or with a different activity, and as much as possible limit the time that they are directly involved with their own child.

As with all aspects of development and behaviour, a consistent approach is vital if children are to benefit from the partnership. It is not just a question of an early years worker knowing that a child needs a rest after lunch, or has a special word that they use when they want to go to the toilet. Parents and carers need to agree on standards of acceptable behaviour, for example, parents may want their child to be encouraged to say 'please' and 'thank you' so the early years workers should respect the wishes of the parents and also encourage this. These standards could be agreed at a meeting in which parents let their wishes be known, and carers explain what is possible, and what and why certain methods could be used.

It could be that during the course of conversations with parents and other professionals, carers are given confidential information, perhaps of a personal nature about the child and their family. It is essential that we regard all information that is given to us as confidential unless we are told otherwise.

CASE STUDY

Jamila is a classroom assistant in a Year I class, which has several children who frequently use inappropriate behaviour ranging from lack of attention to inappropriate language and aggression. Jamila and the teacher have agreed that Jamila will try to manage the behaviour of one child who can be aggressive towards others especially at play and lunch times. Jamila tries to distract the child each time she is aware that he is becoming aggressive and uses praises and reward stickers when he behaves appropriately or achieves. One day at the end of school, a parent comes into the classroom demanding to see Jamila and accuses her of favouritism. The parent claims that her child is never helped in class even though they have reading difficulties, because Jamila is too busy dealing with the naughty ones. The parent claims her child never gets a reward sticker even when they are good and complains that the naughty children get all the good things.

1 Do you think that the parent has a valid point?

2 What can Jamila do?

3 Put yourself into Jamila's position. How could this situation be resolved to the satisfaction of the aggrieved parent and so that the agreed strategy for managing the behaviour of the other child is not compromised?

Communication

Communication is vital if we are to build successful and effective partnerships with parents, carers and other professionals. Communication can be defined as an exchange of ideas, contact between individuals, consultation and interaction. It is also necessary for negotiation, persuasion and in developing and building relationships. Communication is a two-way process that requires a 'giver' and a 'receiver'; it requires time and effort to be effective. Lack of communication can lead to misunderstandings, misinformation and problems in developing a partnership. Communication is a very powerful tool in building and developing partnerships, especially spoken forms of communication. Spoken language can build confidence and trust, but can also destroy confidence and trust.

THINK IT OVER:

At the end of a holiday play scheme, the children and staff put on a show for parents, carers and friends. Ian and Kate went along to support their seven-year-old twins. A casual remark made by one of the play workers over coffee at the end of the show implied that the twins had been unco-operative and 'difficult'. Kate was very upset; Ian was angry and asked the play worker why he hadn't spoken to one of them before. He replied that he thought that the twins might get better over the week. Both parents felt that if there had been difficulties, they should have known about it earlier and could have talked with the twins and sorted something out. In this case, lack of communication had a detrimental effect on the relationship between the parents and the play worker. It also made Kate and Ian think again about sending their children to the play scheme in the future, and Kate admitted that she had feelings of guilt that she had 'naughty children'.

ACTIVITY

There are many different forms of communication. Think of occasions when you have used different forms of communication, for example, have you calmed and communicated with a baby by gently stroking their back, or used your tone of voice to manage a child's behaviour? Record your answers in a table like the one below.

Form of communication	Incident or occasion
Eye contact	
Gestures such as pointing	
Body language	
Tone of voice	
Touch	
Spoken language including listening	
Written language	
Pictures	
Symbols	
Facial expressions	

Body language

Body language is a non-verbal form of communication. Our bodies are giving out messages all the time when we are communicating with another individual.

Sometimes what our body language says is quite different from what the other person actually 'hears' us saying. This can be very detrimental to communication in terms of building a partnership with parents. As much as possible, positive body language should be used when dealing with parents, other professionals and, of course, children.

The table below shows some of the most common forms of body language and some interpretations. However, it must be remembered that these are only possible interpretations and care must be taken not to read too much into another individual's mannerisms. It is a good idea to be familiar with some of the negative forms of body language so that you can, avoid using them.

Body language	Possible interpretation
Erect, brisk walk	Confidence
Standing with hands on hips	Readiness or sometimes aggression
Sitting with legs crossed, foot slightly kicking	Boredom
Arms crossed on chest	Defensiveness
Walking with hands in pockets, shoulders hunched	Dejection
Hand to cheek	Evaluation, thinking
Touching, slightly rubbing nose	Rejection, or doubt, or lying
Rubbing the eye	Disbelief, or doubt
Hands clasped behind back	Anger, frustration, apprehension
Head resting in hand, eyes downcast	Boredom
Rubbing hands	Anticipation
Sitting with hands clasped behind head, legs crossed	Confidence, superiority
Open palm	Sincerity, openness, innocence
Pinching bridge of nose, eyes closed	Negative evaluation
Tapping or drumming fingers	Impatience
Steepling fingers	Authority
Patting or fiddling with hair	Lack of self-confidence, insecurity
Tilted head	Interest
Stroking chin	Trying to make a decision
Looking down, face turned away	Disbelief
Biting nails	Insecurity, nervousness

Some common forms of body language

Listening

We live in an increasingly noisy world; supermarkets play music to persuade us to buy certain products, lifts and trains tell us to 'mind the doors', many homes have constant sounds from CDs, radios and television, not to mention the traffic noise many of us encounter every day. Is there any wonder that at times listening is something that we don't do well? We can easily be distracted when trying to listen to someone and one of the most common complaints from parents is that there is little point trying to talk to childcare workers and/or teachers as they don't listen. Parents have been reported as saying:

> 'I tried to talk to Jess's teacher about Jess crying when I left, but the teacher didn't listen to me and just said that Jess would grow out of it.'
>
> 'I told Tariq's key worker that I was worried about his behaviour, but she didn't hear what I was saying and carried on sorting books.'
>
> 'When I wanted to talk about my child at the end of the day, I was told to make an appointment. I felt that they didn't think my child or I were important.'

A parent who thinks that the practitioner is not listening to them can be unwilling to build a partnership and this will ultimately affect the child. Parents and practitioners could be giving different message to the child, which could confuse them.

It is important to let other people know that we are trying to actively listen to them. This can be done in a variety of ways:

◆ Think about the immediate environment. You will be able to listen more effectively if you and the other person are somewhere quiet, where distractions are reduced, or limited.

◆ Make sure that you have time to listen. There is nothing wrong with suggesting a specific time or making an appointment, provided that the other person understands that this is not a 'brush-off' and that you are doing this to make sure that you will have time to listen to them without interruptions.

◆ Think about your body language. Physically putting yourself at the same level as the other person enables you to have good eye contact, so you should both sit down, or both stand up. Make sure that your gestures are reassuring and positive, such as nodding your head occasionally and not folding your arms across your chest.

Sometimes it is not always possible to plan appointments and specific times for listening, for example, when a distressed parent needs support immediately. However, it is still important to find somewhere quiet and free from distractions and interruptions.

STRATEGIES FOR BECOMING AN EFFECTIVE LISTENER

- ✔ Give the person who is speaking your undivided attention.
- ✔ Ask questions to show that you have listened, want more information or to clarify something that you may not have heard correctly.
- ✔ Summarise what has been said. This makes you listen carefully, lets the person who was speaking know that you have understood what they were saying and reduces the possibility of misunderstandings. This is especially important when discussing aspects of children's behaviour and development.
- ✔ Let the speaker know that you are listening carefully. Maintain eye contact, use appropriate gestures and body language, such as nods of the head, perhaps saying words like 'mmm' or 'yes'.

Spoken language

We use some form of spoken communication every day within our work, our home and social life. Speaking is perhaps one of the most effective forms of communication as spoken words help to build relationships. However, once uttered, words cannot be erased or retracted, so thinking before we speak is often advisable! Spoken language is frequently supplemented with other forms of communication, such as gestures, body language and facial expressions. Communication is most effective when the message is consistent – rather than a person saying one thing but their body language 'saying' something different.

For example, the parent who comes into the room, remains standing and folds their arms is giving a defensive message, but their words might be saying how pleased they are to have the chance to talk to you.

It is very important that we always remember when talking to parents or other professionals that we are discussing a **child**, not a problem. We should focus on what the child can do and their strengths, rather than on what they cannot do. Remember, we are trying to empower the child and help them to manage their own behaviour.

It is also important to respect and acknowledge that parents and other professionals may have different views from our own. This should enable us all to build up a bigger picture of a child through sharing our views and ultimately be in a better position to help the child.

SNAPSHOT

As part of an IEP review Angie made arrangements to speak with Jo's speech therapist. Angie felt that Jo was still having difficulties interacting with his peers and was becoming more frustrated. The speech therapist was, however, very pleased with Jo's progress and felt that he was beginning to understand how to control his breathing and to say sounds. Angie realised that her expectations of Jo were too high and that Jo was actually making progress. As a result of their discussion the next target for Jo focused on him being able to say 'hi', 'yes' and 'no', this was specific, measurable, achievable, relevant and time bound (SMART).

Written language

There is an assumption that professionals are able to write effectively in every situation, such as keeping children's records, planning documents, writing individual education reports and messages for parents. However, this is not always true. Many people have problems with writing effectively and feel uncertain about things like spelling, grammar and punctuation. Remember that it is better to write things simply and correctly than trying to use long words incorrectly in an effort to impress.

There are often times when it is necessary to write down information of a personal nature concerning children and their families. It is important that this information remains confidential, but at the same time parents do have the right of access to written records about their child. However, we should be aware that any written personal information, including data on a computer, is subject to the conditions of the Data Protection Act (2000). Every setting should be registered with the Data Protection Commission (you can get more information from your local government office about how to do this).

Gestures

Many people communicate very effectively using only gestures and signs, for example, people with a hearing impairment. Gestures, like someone's tone of voice, sometimes convey a different message to what is being said. Does shrugging the shoulders mean that we don't know or that we don't care, for example? Gestures, combined with facial expressions and body language, may send very strong messages to others. Many childcare and education workers and parents manage children's behaviour simply by shaking their head combined with a stern 'look', or alternatively convey praise and encouragement with a smile or a 'thumbs up' gesture.

Gestures, like all forms of communication, can convey negative messages. A busy working parent may give a shrug of exasperation when we ask if we can discuss the behaviour of their child at the end of the working day. This should not always be interpreted as the parent not wanting to know or not caring, but possibly that our timing may be at fault and that it may have been better to give the parent a written note or message requesting a meeting at an agreed time.

Touch

The power of positive touches should not be underestimated, but care should be taken to ensure that they are not confused with unwanted or unwelcome touches. A gentle touch can reassure, comfort and calm, especially with a distressed parent, but may be interpreted by some as intrusive and unwanted. It is good practice to remember that not everyone responds well to 'touchy-feely' people; if you are in doubt, do not reach out to touch a parent or carer.

Pictures and symbols

We are surrounded by pictures and symbols which are used in everyday life to convey messages and communicate. Symbols are the foundation of reading and writing. We introduce young children to symbols such as circles and squares usually before we introduce them to letter shapes, and advertisers use pictures and symbols to persuade us to buy certain products. However, pictures and symbols can sometimes be misleading. Look at the pictures and symbols below – what do you think the message is?

How would you interpret these symbols? 'Time for play?' Or 'Watches for children?'
Or even 'Four clocks per child?'

Lee is George's key worker and he is becoming concerned about some aspects of George's behaviour. Lee decides to ask George's father if they can get together to talk about George. When they meet, George's father is very defensive and says that his son is just going through a normal phase. He ends the conversation by saying that Lee doesn't know what he is talking about, as what sort of 'proper' man would do a job like his.

1 If you were Lee, what would you do next?

2 What communication strategies could Lee use when he meets George's father in the future?

Possible barriers to developing a partnership with parents and carers

Many parents are incredibly busy people and simply do not have the time to stop and discuss their child frequently. This should not be interpreted as not caring or being interested about their child. For such parents it is often better to make a fixed appointment at an agreed time to discuss their child. In this way the parent knows what is expected of them and will have more respect for the professional childcare worker as they seem to understand the needs and demands of the parents.

On the other hand, childcare workers are also very busy individuals and cannot always be available for parents 'on demand'. There could be times when talking to a parent is inconvenient and stops them from being with other children. In such circumstances, the childcare worker should politely suggest to the parent that they either talk to another available member of staff or come back and talk at a mutually convenient time. Never jeopardise the safety and well-being of children.

Dealing with stressed parents

Sometimes parents under stress find it difficult to manage their children's behaviour and maintain a partnership with teachers and carers. Stress is caused by many different factors and everyone reacts to it in different ways. It is important that early years workers are aware of stressful situations and are able to support parents, either by being able to give information about other agencies or professionals that may help, or by listening and talking to parents – without passing opinions or judgements about them. For example, financial difficulties may cause depression and poor health. Whilst early years and childcare workers cannot offer a family more money, they can help the family to access support and perhaps benefits.

Similarly, unemployment may cause stress as parents may feel inadequate and lack confidence. Changes in circumstances, such as changing jobs, moving home or a breakdown in family relationships, may all cause stress and affect the way parents relate and react to their children's carers and teachers. Many parents feel socially isolated and may not feel able to establish relationships with other parents, teachers and carers. This could be a result of not understanding the language, or having a 'reputation' that has prompted a negative reaction from other people, such as a violent partner or a family member who is in prison. In such circumstances, early years and childcare workers can suggest support networks that may be able to help.

ACTIVITY

Think about setting up a file of information for parents about services and agencies that can help them. The file could simply be a list of names, addresses, websites and telephone numbers sorted into different categories, such as housing, health issues support groups, benefits.

1 What benefits can you think of for your workplace in setting up a parent's information file?

2 What benefits can you think of for parents in having access to an information file?

Language as a barrier to communication

Differences in language can make working in partnership with parents difficult. Not every parent is fluent in the language used by their child's teacher or early years worker. Some parents may have visual or hearing impairments. Interpreters and signers can be used, and staff could be encouraged to learn some simple sign language, especially greetings.

People with speech impediments often become very frustrated when well-meaning individuals 'speak' for them and invariably get the meaning completely wrong. Be patient and calm and wait for the other person to speak as you would do for anyone else.

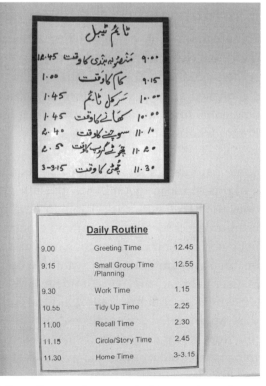

Information can be presented in a variety of ways

Physical barriers to communication

If settings want to work in partnership with parents then it is important that there is somewhere, other than the doorstep, where staff and parents can talk. Physical hindrances, such as lack of space, may be intimidating for some parents. It is not good practice to discuss a child's inappropriate behaviour with their parents in full view and earshot of everyone else. Many schools and early years settings have security systems to prevent unwanted visitors,

Making the setting welcoming to parents will encourage communication

but these may also hinder an open-door policy. In such cases, staff will have to work hard to reassure parents that they are welcome into the setting.

Emotional barriers to communication

Some parents have a fear of educational and care settings, perhaps because of their own experiences, or they may feel hostile towards the staff, particularly if it is their child who always seems to be in 'trouble'. A partnership can still be established and lines of communication kept open through newsletters, occasional telephone calls (especially to give good news and praise) and home/school/nursery books.

Some parents do not share the aims of a setting when developing a partnership, and this can lead to conflict with staff. There may be many reasons why a parent does not agree with the setting, for example, the parents and child may have been ordered by a court to attend a particular setting, or the parent may not believe that their child has behaved in a particular way; they may feel resentful or threatened and may not want to work in partnership. In such circumstances it is essential that early years and childcare workers do not become judgemental or close lines of communication. It is important that staff take time to explain why they do things in certain ways. Sometimes just giving out a prospectus or brochure is not enough and many settings invite parents to workshops, information talks and social events that are designed to be relaxed, informal and non-threatening.

CASE STUDY

Jen hated maths at school and believed that she couldn't do it at all. Her son has started nursery and already Jen thinks that he is better than her and feels very inadequate. The nursery have organised a series of 'curriculum' evenings for parents to try to explain the Foundation Stage. Jen plucks up the courage to go to the evening on mathematical development. She is greeted by her son's key worker and offered a cup of coffee. She is then invited to 'play in the sand tray' with two other parents. There is lots of chatter and laughter and Jen becomes more relaxed and is able to join in with more play activities. She leaves feeling more positive about maths than she has in a long time.

1. How else could the nursery staff help Jen?
2. Why is it important for the nursery staff to try to build on Jen's positive experience?

Partnerships as a means of support for parents

Most partnerships with parents develop smoothly, with the interests and needs of the child being the 'cornerstones'. Many parents become stressed, distressed or even angry when they realise that their child is causing concern. However, when parents are stressed for whatever reason, the partnership may be their only means of support. In such circumstances, tact, sensitivity and professional knowledge and understanding must be used in order to maintain the partnership. From time to time, parents seek advice and guidance about the behaviour of their children from early years professionals. It is essential that any information given to parents is accurate and up to date. Stressful situations can be made worse and partnerships irreparably damaged by giving incorrect information.

Parents are the first educators of their children. Parents know their own children better than anyone else and have a wealth of information to share with early years workers. We can have access to this information if there is effective communication with parents, and partnerships are based upon mutual respect and understanding. Similarly, the key to dealing effectively with children's behaviour is an understanding of how to meet their needs through communication and partnership with other professionals, the parents and the children themselves.

CHECKPOINT

1. The Children Act (1989) gave parents more rights: true or false?
2. What is meant by authoritarian parenting?
3. List three examples of family structures.
4. Give two key features of an effective settling-in policy.
5. List three forms of communication.
6. List three things that could make communication and/or developing a partnership difficult.
7. Who are the first educators of children?
8. How would you define a partnership?

Key figures in the study of behaviour

Theorist	Date	Main area of study	Main features
Chris Athey		Cognitive development	Developed the concept of schemas.
Albert Bandura	1925–	Social learning	Studied how children learn from role models and how this can influence their behaviour.
John Bowlby	1907–1990	Attachment	Looked at the effects of forming strong bonds and attachments. Work was continued by James and Joyce Robertson and strongly influenced the care of children in hospitals and institutions.
Jerome Bruner	1915–	Scaffolding	Built on the ideas of Vygotsky but developed the idea that children develop different ways of thinking rather than passing through stages. Considered the role of the adult in helping children learn.
Noam Chomsky	1928–	Language development	Introduced the idea of a language acquisition device (LAD) which was instinctive. Can be linked to the nature/nurture debate.
Erik Erikson	1902–1994	Emotional and personality development	A student of Freud; felt that emotional and social development are linked to cognitive and language development. Personality continues to develop into adulthood. Stages of development are called psychosocial as children explore relationships.
Sigmund Freud	1856–1939	Emotional and personality development	First theorist to consider the unconscious mind and its effects and influences on behaviour. Believed development is stage-like, stages are called psychosexual and are linked to the physical pleasures associated with each stage.
Friedrich Froebel	1782–1852	Early learning through play	Established the first Kindergarten, believed in indoor and outdoor play and placed great value on symbolic behaviour.

Theorist	Date	Main area of study	Main features
Arnold Gesell	1880–1961	Maturation	Described patterns of development that are genetically programmed.
William Glasser	1925–	Needs	Believed in empowering children through non-judgemental recognition leading to a positive feeling of self-worth.
Susan Isaacs	1885–1948	Value of parents and play	Influenced by Froebel. Believed that play would enable children to have a balanced view of life. Parents are the main educators of children.
Lawrence Kohlberg	1927–1987	Moral development and gender identity	Extended and redefined Piaget's views. Suggested that individuals develop moral reasoning in six stages at three levels. Sex-roles emerge as stage-like development in cognition.
Abraham Maslow	1908–1970	Needs	Developed a hierarchy of needs that follow the life cycle. The hierarchy has five levels and is dynamic, with the dominant need always shifting.
Margaret McMillan	1860–1931	First-hand learning and free play	Member of the Froebel Society. Believed in training for early years workers.
Maria Montessori	1870–1952	Structured play	Believed children have times in their lives when they are more able to learn certain things than at other times.
Ivan Pavlov	1849–1936	Classical conditioning	Studied a type of learning where an automatic response such as a reflex is triggered by a new stimulus. Worked with dogs.
Jean Piaget	1896–1980	Cognitive and language development, also play and moral understanding	Introduced the theory of stages of cognitive development, considered how children learn concepts. Also considered stages of play and moral development. Highly influential.
B. F. Skinner	1904–1990	Behaviourist theory	Worked with animals, remembered for the 'Skinner Box' and introduced the idea that behaviour would be repeated if it was reinforced.
Rudolf Steiner	1861–1925	Community education	Believed relationships between children and adults are very important if a child is to develop to their full potential.
Edward Thorndike	1874–1949	Reinforcement	Followed work of Skinner. Assumed that learning happens due to an association being made between a stimulus and a response and the pleasure that follows.
Lev Vygotsky	1896–1934	Social learning	Worked along similar lines to Piaget in that he believed children are active learners, but also upheld that social development is a very important part of cognitive development. Introduced the idea of the zone of proximal development (ZPD).

Chapter 1

1 Core characteristics are moulded by the experiences of childhood and the influence of the family.

2 Factors that influence our views and values are:
- ◆ Culture and ethnicity
- ◆ Religion
- ◆ Age
- ◆ Education
- ◆ Gender
- ◆ Family structures and upbringing.

3 Punishments do not consider the reasons for the behaviour.

4 Empowerment suggest that children should be supported to mange their own behaviour, and be encouraged to learn the skills and abilities to discipline themselves.

5 Empowerment is often associated with teaching children effective strategies to protect them from many forms of abuse.

6 A multi-professional approach to meeting the needs of children has been prompted by the Children Act (1989).

7 Sure Start uses a multi-professional approach.

Chapter 2

1 Classical conditioning is when an unconscious response is triggered by a new stimulus after the new stimulus has been associated with or paired with the usual stimulus that triggers that response. Pavlov is the most famous theorist associated with classical conditioning.

2 A reflex action is the start of classical conditioning. It is an innate, involuntary action or behaviour that is brought about by an antecedent event.

3   Extinction can be defined as the non-production of a response when a conditioned stimulus is presented. It relates to Pavlov's theory of classical conditioning.

4   Shaping involves breaking down a new skill into small manageable steps, with each step achieved reinforced with praise. So to teach a child to play an instrument you could start with teaching how to hold the instrument, or position the hands, followed by how to move one or two fingers; when this is successfully achieved more complex movements involving either more fingers or both hands could be introduced.

5   Positive role models are an intrinsic aspect of social learning theory.

6   The five processes are: motivation, attention, practice, memory, frequent revisiting.

7   Cognitive theory is concerned with thought; it is also known as constructivist theory. Piaget, Kohlberg, Bruner and Vygotsky are all cognitive/constructivist theorists.

8   A schema is a basic thought, concept or idea about the environment. An example of a schema could be anything that a child already knows and is able to build upon.

9   The Zone of Proximal Development allows a child, with appropriate adult help, to achieve at a higher level than they would be able to do unaided.

Chapter 3

1   Sigmund Freud and Erik Erikson.

2   Freud suggested that the first element of personality development is the id, followed by the ego and finally the superego.

3   Children could become ashamed of their perceived 'failure' and so develop poor self-esteem and low self-confidence.

4   Self-image can be influenced by the role that you have within your family.

5   John Bowlby developed the theory of attachment and as a result new mothers are encouraged to hold and bond with their babies as soon as possible after birth.

6   The stages of separation are:

    a   protest

    b   despair

    c   detachment.

7   Kohlberg suggested that this would be children of primary school and early secondary school age.

8 A self-fulfilling prophecy can be interpreted as giving a person a label, such as 'naughty' or 'good', which becomes the way that they believe they are expected to behave.

Chapter 4

1 The first level of Maslow's hierarchy is concerned with meeting basic physiological needs. These needs are dominant in a newborn baby. As the child grows they become more mobile and so safety and security needs are important. Children need to socialise at toddler and pre-school groups, nurseries and schools, so the need to be accepted and belong to a group is important. The need for self-esteem and a feeling of worth is dominant in children and adolescents. The need to reach the self-actualisation stage does not usually happen until later in life.

2 The first level of Maslow's hierarchy is basic physiological or survival needs; the baby or young child is reliant on their main carer to meet those needs.

3 They will become irritable and may show aggressive forms of behaviour.

4 Freud's defence mechanisms are:
   a repression
   b rationalising
   c projection
   d displacement
   e sublimation.

5 Internal needs are self-respect, autonomy and achievement.

6 If an individual is unable to satisfy the need for esteem through constructive and appropriate behaviour and actions.

7 Breakfast clubs meet the physiological needs, especially for food and water, (or a drink).

8 An undernourished child may have poor concentration levels, be listless and appear tired.

9 This could be by *doing*, a physical activity, so if physiological needs are not met, development could be affected and limit physical activity.

10 When behaviour is dominated by physiological needs, a child may display these behaviours if they think their needs are not being met.

Chapter 5

1 Children were regarded as part of adult society, the only difference being that they were smaller than adults.

2 One of the main impacts of this philanthropic approach was that large numbers of children were left with nothing to do and no income.

3 Mechanical teaching, rote-learning and strict authoritarian discipline were encouraged.

4 The Children Act (1908).

5 The Geneva Declaration in 1924.

6 Sowing the seeds of empowerment.

7 The Convention states that children have a right to good food, shelter, education and play, the right to say what they think and to be listened to and the right from protection from abuse.

8 The phrase is 'the needs of the children are paramount'.

9 Standard 11.

10 Four reasons are:

　a Is it right for another person to be violent towards another – the moral issue.

　b Smacking teaches children that it is acceptable to be aggressive.

　c Smacking does not teach children how to resolve problems or conflicts in a peaceful way.

　d Many young children do not understand the reasons why they have been smacked.

Chapter 6

1 Nature is those aspects of our development that are genetically inherited. Nurture is those aspects that are influenced by the environment in which we grow and develop.

2 Some children may feel that the expectations are too high, and they may feel worthless, unloved and very inadequate about their own abilities.

3 Research shows that second or middle-born children adopt characteristics and behaviours that are the exact opposite of the first-born, and may regarded as trouble-makers, especially if the first-born is co-operative and compliant.

4 At around thirty months.

5 Siblings may feel jealous, guilty about negative thoughts and attitudes, anxious, demanding and attention-seeking.

6 Parents are now involved as much as possible, play therapists work alongside medical staff and named nurses work with specific children.

7 If the expectations of the group are different to those of parents, carers or the school.

8 Bullying can be:

◆ name-calling

◆ verbal abuse

◆ fighting

◆ physical attacks

◆ not allowing a child to participate in activities

◆ racial remarks

◆ discriminatory remarks

◆ threats.

9 The four forms of abuse are:

◆ physical

◆ sexual

◆ neglect

◆ emotional/psychological.

10 Desensitisation is when an individual gradually accepts violence and aggressive behaviours as normal events in everyday life, due to over-exposure to such events in the media, for example, television programmes.

Chapter 7

1 The behaviourist theory.

2 Being involved in this way helps children to understand the reasons for the boundaries, and this kind of understanding is part of empowerment.

3 Offering children choices, encouraging children to make decisions, giving praise, recognition and positive reinforcement and playing games where children are given control of situations are all ways (but not the only ways) of empowering children.

4 Amber behaviours are caution behaviours that are a result of children still learning boundaries, or behaviours displayed during a temporary developmental regression.

5 The child could interpret this as you not loving them at all.

6 Simple rules are easier to remember, therefore they are more likely to be effective.

7 A consistent approach with children reassures them, because then they know what the boundaries and, if appropriate, what the rules are.

8 If they feel that they are not in control of a situation.

9 In the psychoanalytical theories of Freud.

10 When playing instruments, children need to listen to one another, respond to the cues of others and take turns. These are all part of the development of social skills.

Chapter 8

1 It is based on the theory of operant conditioning.

2 **A**ntecedents, **B**ehaviour and **C**onsequences

3 Through observation, assessment and by talking to the child and their parents/carers.

4 This description is not factual; it is emotional and does not describe what the child actually does.

5 You could have listed things such as: satisfaction, pleasure, attention from others (adults and children), guilt feelings, feelings of power over another child or adult.

6 It is important because it helps to focus on positive things about the child, what they can do and what they are good at.

7 Specific, Measurable, Achievable, Relevant and Time-bound.

8 An achievable target allows a child to succeed, it empowers them and helps them to develop self-confidence and self-esteem.

Chapter 9

1 Team goals; participation; team decision-making and team member resources.

2 Special Educational Needs Co-ordinator.

3 There are three stages in the graduated approach in the Code of Practice for the Identification and Assessment of Children with Special Educational Needs.

4 Primary health care teams are usually made up of general practitioners (GPs), health visitors, community midwives and nurses.

5 Sure Start aims to help parents, parents-to-be and children to access support, advice on nurturing, health services and early learning.

6 False. Family centres are set up by local social service departments.

7 An educational psychologist specialises in the way children learn.

8 A clinical psychologist plans and develops programmes of behaviour modification or therapy that will be implemented by the child's family and nursery or school.

9 Standard 11 of the National Standards concerns behaviour and states that adults caring for children in any setting must be able to manage a wide range of children's behaviour in a way that promotes their welfare and development.

Chapter 10

1 True.

2 Authoritarian parents are more likely to attempt to manage, limit and control the behaviour of their children and will explain the 'rules'.

3 Family structures can be:

   ◆ adoptive

- extended
- nomadic
- reconstituted
- mixed ethnic background
- nuclear
- single-parent
- homosexual.

4   Key features of an effective settling-in policy might be:

- prior pre-arranged visits to the setting
- parents and children attending together at the beginning
- lack of pressure on the parents to leave their child too soon
- clear guidelines for the less confident parent to follow when settling their child
- gradual decrease in time spent with parent in the setting.

5   Communication can be through:

- pictures
- symbols
- eye contact
- gestures
- body language
- tone of voice
- touch
- spoken language
- written language.

6   Difficulties can be caused by:

- fear
- lack of time
- physical hindrances
- stress
- language difficulties.

7   Parents are children's first educators.

8   A partnership is a joint relationship, a collaboration, a sharing of ideas and expertise.

References and further reading

Barnard, H. C. (1969) *A History of English Education*, London: University of London Press

Bull, J. et al. (1994) *Implementing the Children Act for Children Under 8*, London: HMSO

Bowlby, J. (reprinted 1990) *Child Care and the Growth of Love*, London: Penguin Books

Bruce, T. (1997) *Early Childhood Education*, London: Hodder and Stoughton

CACHE (2002) *Level 3 Candidate Handbook for the Diploma in Play Work*, CACHE

Daehler, M. and Bukatko, D. (1992) *Child Development*, Boston: Houghton and Mifflin

Davenport, G. (1994) *An Introduction to Child Development*, London: Collins Educational

Dewar, J. (1992) *Law and the Family*, London: Butterworth Heinemann

DfES/Sure Start (2002) *Birth to Three Matters* DfES

Donaldson, M. (1987) *Children's Minds*, London: Fontana Press

'Including special children' September 2002, Questions Publishing

'Including special children' March 2003, Questions Publishing

Jarvis, M. and Chandler, E. (2001) *Angles on Child Psychology*, Cheltenham: Nelson Thornes

Kamen, T. (2000) *Psychology for Childhood Studies*, London: Hodder and Stoughton

Lee, V. and Das Gupta, P. (1998) *Children's Cognitive and Language Development*, Oxford: Blackwell in association with Open University Press

Merret, F. and Whedall, K. (1990) *Positive Teaching in the Primary School*, London: Paul Chapman Publishing

Mukherji, P. (1996) *Understanding Young Children's Behaviour*, Cheltenham: Nelson Thornes

Murphy, M. (1995) *Working Together In Child Protection*, Aldershot: Ashgate Publishing

Nursery World May 2002, TSL Publications Ltd

Nursery World April 2003, TSL Publications Ltd

Rodd, J. (1996) *Understanding Young Children's Behaviour*, St. Leonards: Allen and Unwin

Tassoni, P. (2003) *Supporting Special Needs: Understanding Inclusion in the Early Years*, Oxford: Heinemann

Teachers March 2003, DfES

Whiting, B. B. and Edwards C. P. (1988) *Children of Different Worlds*, Cambridge: Harvard University Press

Woolfson, R. (1995) *Understanding Children* Caring Books

Working together to safeguard children September 2000, The National Assembly for Wales

Wyse, D. and Hawtin, A. (2000) *Children – A multi-professional perspective*, London: Arnold Publishers

Useful addresses and websites

Many of the details below are for each organisation's head office, which should be able to provide local contact numbers.

ADD/ADHD Family Support group
1a The High Street
Dilton Marsh
Nr Westbury
Wiltshire BA13 4DL
Tel: 01373 826045

British Association for Counselling and Psychotherapy
1 Regent Place
Rugby
Warwickshire   CV21 2PJ
Tel: 0870 443 5252
Web: www.bac.co.uk

British Dyslexia Association
98 London Road
Reading RG1 5AU
Tel: 0118 966 8271
Email: info@dyslexiahelp-bda.demon.co.uk
Web: www.bda-dyslexia.org.uk

British Society of Music Therapy
69 Avondale
Barnet
Hertfordshire EN4 8NB
Tel: 0181 368 8879

Childline
Studd Street
London N1 0QW
Tel: 08001111
Web: www.childline.org.uk

Compassionate Friends
53 North Street
Bristol
BS3 1EN
Tel: 0117 966 5202

To obtain the National Standards for Under-Eights Day Care and Childminding 2001, apply to:
DfES Publications
PO Box 5050 Sherwood Park
Anneseley
Nottingham
NG15 0DJ

Good Grief
Grindstone Manor Mews
Horrabridge
Yelverton
Devon PL20 7QY
Tel: 01822 854358

Kidscape
2 Grosvenor Gardens
London SW1W 0DH
Tel: 020 7730 3300
Email: webinfo@kidscape.ork.uk
Web: www.kidscape.org.uk

National Council for One Parent Families
255 Kentish Town Road
London NW4 2LX
Tel: 0800 018 5026
Web: www.oneparentfamilies.org.uk

National Drugs Helpline
Telephone 0800 77 66 00
Email: helpline@ndh.org.uk
Web: www.ndh.org.uk

Parentline Plus
520 Highgate Studios
53-79 Highgate Road
Kentish Town
London NW5 1TL
Tel: 020 7284 5500
Web: www.parentlinelpus.org.uk

Parents Advice Centre
Franklin House
12 Brunswick Street
Belfast BT2 7GE
Tel: 028 9023 8800
Email: Belfast@pachelp.org.uk
Web: www.parentsadvicecentre.org.uk

The Dyspraxia Foundation
8 West Alley
Hitchin
Hertfordshire SG5 1EG
Tel: 01462 454986

The Sickle Cell Society
54 Station Road
Harelesdon
London NW10 4UA
Tel: 020 8961 77795
Email: sickleinfoline@btinternet.com
Web: sicklecell.org.uk

The National Autistic Society
393 City Road
London EC1V 1NG
Tel: 020 7833 2299
Email: nas@nas.org.uk
Web: www.oneworld.org/autism_uk

Index